The *Magic* of *Saying Yes*

Answering Your Heart's True Calling

Betsy Gutting

New Bloom Press
Seattle, WA

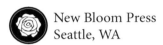 New Bloom Press
Seattle, WA

Cover Design: Kate Warinsky

Cover Photo: Kate Warinsky

Interior Book Design: Amy Pogue

Library of Congress Cataloging-in-Publication Data:

Gutting, Betsy
The Magic of Saying Yes: Answering Your Heart's True Calling, 1st ed.
ISBN 978-0-9889159-0-9
1. Personal Growth 2. Self-Actualization 3. Spirituality

First edition paperback: March 2013

1 2 3 4 5 6 7 8 9 10

Printed in the United States of America

For Kate and Molly,
whose sheer presence lights me up.
Always trust your heart.

Contents

Introduction

This book is about freeing yourself to follow your heart.

I once stood where you are now. I found myself in the self-growth/spirituality section, searching for clues and answers to my life's direction. Perhaps like you, I was "in transition," wrestling with potentially life-altering decisions.

My quest centered on discovering my passion, purpose, and right livelihood. Then my marriage started to shift. Alternating between feelings of restlessness and angst, I sincerely (and sometimes desperately) desired to know what was next, but I had no idea how to find it.

This is the book I needed then.

You, too, may deeply desire clarity about one or more areas of your life. Your life may seem fine enough, but perhaps you are feeling flat and wondering if you are missing out on something more. Or you may be suffering a shattering loss, looking for a lifeline and a practical plan for finding comfort and moving forward. It is also possible that you are feeling called to take a step that feels bold, scary, or unpopular. You are looking for permission, confidence, and the courage to say yes anyway. If you see yourself in any of these scenarios, I wrote this book for you.

When it felt as though my life was unraveling, I needed to know that I was not alone. I needed reassurance that I was not the only person suffering from confusion, doubt, and pain brought on by the fear of an uncertain future. I needed to hear my story in someone else's story, someone who had been where I was, who had found and followed their own truth and lived to joyfully share their lessons and successes with others. This is why you will hear my story and the stories of some of my clients in these pages. Hearing your story in someone else's story is a necessary and powerful healing balm.

A word about privacy: I have changed the names of all clients, some friends, and one location in order to protect privacy. Spiritual mentors, teachers, and other friends appear with their original names. Regardless of the names used, all of the facts and circumstances are told with complete truth and accuracy.

A Practical Guidebook

This book is not only meant to comfort, inspire, and empower you with stories. It is a practical guidebook for your own journey. In the reflection exercises, practices, and guided meditations, I offer you the same methods that have freed my coaching clients to say yes to their dreams. Taken together, these processes offer a map and an itinerary—a plan you can follow that will give you a solid structure to hold and contain your places of uncertainty.

To encourage you, I provide space in the book for you to write your responses to the reflective exercises. I suggest that you also keep a spiral notebook or journal close by, in case you need additional room.

By fully engaging in these processes, you will come to trust the wise place inside of you that has your answers. I call it your soul, but you can call it anything you like. Whatever you name it, the practical and powerful tools in these pages will help you to forge an intimate and sacred bond with your most faithful and trustworthy guide.

Discovering your heart's true calling asks for your full engagement and participation. If I told you that I was going to teach you how to ride a bike from a step-by-step diagram, you might laugh. Similarly, partnering with your wise and unconditionally-loving, divine connection cannot be taught—it can only be experienced. You will forge this life-enhancing connection by participating actively in the exercises and practices. You may feel like avoiding some practices; I suggest you do them anyway. Often the ones you resist the most have the greatest potential to positively transform you. It is common, as well, to receive revealing insights from some exercises and little from others. Keep your eye on the prize and continue forward. Your dedication to the process will bring the incredible reward of awakening you to your passion, your power, and your divine destiny. The skills you learn will give you the ability and inner strength to move through life's inevitable bumps and losses. This is your ticket to feeling free to create the life *you* choose.

An Invitation to Adventure

You may be skeptical that you, too, could access this wisdom and direction within yourself. This is natural and understandable, especially if you're in the midst of painful change or crisis. You do not have to believe in the methods I offer in this book for them to usher you forward. They are in harmony with spiritual law. If you work the tools, they will work for you, whether you believe in them or not. You only need a sincere desire and willingness to hear and follow your heart's true calling.

No matter what your current circumstances, this book will guide you to imagine a brand new life chapter—and a new you—beyond what you have ever before experienced. Not despite your feelings of angst or loss or something missing, but because of them. These feelings are catalysts to your awakening. Your destiny is calling you to wake up to your authentic nature—to step into the shape that has been patiently waiting for you all along.

There is a magic to saying yes. By magic I don't mean positive or magical thinking. I am talking about something that has to be experienced to be known. When you say yes to the pull of a vision, a message from your soul, or the passion ignited by your sincere heart's desire, you open a door through which universal assistance flows to you. This is *real* magic. You will find your path to your own magical yes in these pages.

This book is meant to take you on a transformational adventure—to cross the bridge from where you are now to where you would like to be. Whether or not you are aware of it in this moment, you are the powerful co-creator of your own life. You are poised to activate your own inner magician to experience the alchemy of releasing the past and welcoming a new beginning.

I invite you to take my hand and walk with me across the bridge from uncertainty and confusion into clarity, confidence, and calm. I will lead you through your own journey of realizing your passion and purpose. I will help you hear and answer your heart's true calling. In my experience, there is no more exquisite or worthy endeavor. I am with you all the way.

Betsy Gutting
Seattle, Washington

1

 # Becoming Real

Just trust yourself, and then you will know how to live.

~ Johann Wolfgang von Goethe

There is nothing you need to do but open your heart, see what you see, and feel what you feel. Let it in. Speak your true voice. You are already there. You are so ready to fly!

~ A Journal Entry

"I wish I'd had the courage to live a life true to myself, not the life others expected of me." This is the number one regret people express as they near the end of their lives, reports Bronnie Ware, who counseled people in their last weeks of life and who chronicles her story in *The Top Five Regrets of the Dying*.[1]

When I read this quote at the beginning of my workshops, the room invariably becomes very still as participants experience a sense of deep recognition. I believe this is because we all long to live true to ourselves. We each yearn to fulfill our destiny, even if we don't know what this thing we call destiny looks like. We can feel this longing as a part of our innate wiring. This yearning or hunger for more is our destiny's way of getting our attention. It is our spirit's way of waking us up to come alive, take life in our arms, and say yes to what we truly desire.

I never in my wildest imagination expected I would be a practicing intuitive life coach. Or that I would write a book about saying yes to your heart's desire. The truth is, I thought I was happy living a reasonably comfortable life, busy working as a new lawyer, married to a decent man, and raising two spirited daughters in a serene, tree-lined, bedroom neighborhood of Seattle.

But one day, my view of my seemingly good life collapsed when I woke up to a deeper truth. In my work as a lawyer, there was a palpable something missing. I worked with kind, lovely people, but researching and writing legal briefs day in and day out was beginning to feel like a life sentence. Am I in the right place? Is this all there is? I had to ask myself. At the time, however, I had no clue *what* was missing.

I only sensed that a big part of me—my exuberant, fully alive, and authentic self—was getting very short shrift. I saw no place for my creative voice in the daily practice of law. At work, I suppressed my playful zest for life. There was no room to express my deeper, loving heart. Fun had been relegated to weekends or vacations. Meanwhile, my dutiful, good-girl self was showing up and doing all the right things to make this sensible, secure career work. But the part of me that sparked my inspiration and gave me heart-skipping joy, my inner creative child—she had moved out of my life completely.

If you're reading this book, you may be in the throes of change or transition. Someone or something in your life may have pulled the proverbial rug out from underneath you. You may be experiencing depression, inertia, fear, a scary medical diagnosis, chronic anxiety, or deep despair.

Or you may be feeling that your current relationship or job no longer fits you, as though you are showing up and going through the motions like a stranger in your own life. Something is missing but you don't necessarily know the fullness of what it is. You may feel numb, empty, restless, or anxious to break free while still holding yourself back—trapped with no clear way through—as though you are driving with the emergency brake on.

Chaos and confusion always precede clarity. Having moved through and helped my clients navigate these very same emotions and circumstances over the past eleven years, I can say this with absolute certainty: there is a wise place inside of you that knows your truth and has your answers.

You are not alone. It is my sincere intention and joy to guide you in these pages to your own wise knowing. My desire is to help free you to follow your heart.

You might be thinking, Wait—I don't even know what my heart wants. What *do* I desire? What *is* my truth?

First, let me explain how I discovered mine.

In the midst of my own career angst and restlessness, I began soul-searching. It scared me to think about giving up my hard-earned career. I felt confident that I could craft strong legal arguments. But what else could I be this good at? Was there anything that would light me up and keep me passionately engaged?

And who in their right mind would throw away all that training and financial investment anyway?

I had no answers to these questions. I only knew that where I was, was not where I wanted to be.

In a red spiral notebook, I began scrawling the question: *What is my passion? If not law, then what* is *it?*

I continued daily journaling. I kept asking the question. Something inside me knew there was more—even if I didn't know what it looked like.

Then one night around 3 a.m., I was literally awoken by the powerful intensity of a vividly lifelike dream. Just the evening before, I had signed a contract in my journal with Spirit, my name for wise inner guidance and my higher power. In this contract, I sincerely committed to finding my passion. I agreed that I would follow the signs and synchronicities—the inner nudges from my divine guide. "Just tell me what to do!" I had practically begged. "Give me a sign. Give me some—any—direction."

In vivid Technicolor, I saw myself deliver a stand-up comedy routine for a real, live audience. All the elements were there: a small, black stage backed by a red velvet curtain; a dark, smoke-filled bar; and me, spontaneously connecting with the audience.

And they were laughing!

Believe me, I had never before entertained even the shred of a thought of being a comedian. I think I'd been to maybe two comedy clubs in my entire life. I'd been a shy, sensitive child, and my only acting experience consisted of a nonspeaking chorus part in one high school musical for which I'd moved through earth-shaking fear just to audition. Clearly, nothing in my past had prepared me for this gigantic leap into the comedic unknown. I was definitely not qualified.

"Nooo!" I shouted inside, as my husband lay peacefully ignorant next to his frantic wife. "I cannot do this!"

"Too late," I felt Spirit gently nudge, "you've already signed the contract."

"What if I could actually be funny?" I heard a quiet yet turned-on voice inside say. The vision of me onstage, alone, terrified me. But it was also exhilarating to imagine that I could possibly pull it off.

The dream was so powerful that it felt like an answer from my soul. This was not the kind of dream that quietly passes through your consciousness and slips away after your morning coffee. It felt like a get-into-action wake-up call from a deeper part of me. The thought of following this guidance ignited my passion and my fear at the same time, creating what I've come to call *exhilarated fear*, a sign that contains the message, *this is incredibly scary, but I just know I have to do it anyway.*

Too restless to return to sleep, I began scrawling raw joke material onto the pages of my dream journal. My whole body began to buzz with the excitement of taking on this challenge. My passion came from the pipe-dream possibility that maybe I *could* actually make an audience laugh.

What if this were possible? What if I could, even momentarily, succeed at this endeavor? The more I imagined myself being engagingly funny on stage, the more I felt my passionate potential expand. I didn't realize it then, but the small act of writing a few attempts at punch lines actually began moving me toward a new vision of myself. In saying yes, a new, more empowered, me was slowly beginning to emerge.

Two days later, a continuing education flyer came in the mail, advertising an upcoming class for *Beginning Stand-Up Comedy*. What are the chances of this kind of class being offered within weeks of my dream—seriously?! This was *beyond* a sign or synchronicity—it felt more like a *mandate* from Spirit to say yes.

Six other hopeful comics and I showed up to learn how to hold a microphone and write funny "bits" with guidance from our warm and able teacher. In the fourth week of class, we took turns walking into the fire, entertaining a supportive audience of family and friends. Encouragement from seasoned comedians on amateur open mic nights kept me going. I was soon landing professional gigs.

Saying yes to the call to try stand-up comedy was changing my life, although I didn't know this was happening at the time. I was too busy trying to keep up with Spirit, a force that seemed to keep pulling me toward a vision that I couldn't yet see the big picture of. Each night on stage, I faced the fear of needing to be funny or "bomb." It was like walking on blistering hot coals every time. Then when the audience did laugh, which often surprised me, I would float on feelings of elation for hours afterward.

I began to experience what it felt like to be in the creative flow. Inspired new material came to me in my sleepy state just before getting out of bed, or through my morning journaling. My kids were my muses, too, saying the funniest things that gave me great stories to try onstage. Every time I got an idea for a new punch line, I felt a delightful shiver down my spine. "Oh my gosh, something really great just came to me. What do you think—do you think this is funny?" I was constantly calling my husband, mother, best friend—whoever would listen—to run my inspiration of the moment by them.

How could this be happening? I had no training in comedy or crafting humor writing. I began to see that I was not creating alone. I discovered that I was intimately connected to unseen forces that were truly guiding me.

This one single dream ignited a huge spark in my heart.

It woke me up.

I awakened to a new reality—that there was so much more to me than my own ideas of what was possible. I had read that the Universe was conspiring for my success, and I began to witness this truth. All of a sudden, my livelihood and life were no longer limited or defined by my past training, degrees, or resume. I realized, now seeing with *real eyes*, that I had vast creative potential I had barely tapped into. I had talents that could be nourished and developed by signing on with my soul as my wise guide.

My comedy stint lit the fire in my belly. As much as I felt ignited by the adventure of performing, I was still a mom of young, school-age daughters. The late nights of emceeing comedy shows until 2 a.m. became physically exhausting. I so loved connecting with an audience, but I also wanted a good night's sleep, and working in smoky bars was getting old.

My passion for living a fully authentic life kept propelling me forward. *If telling funny stories in comedy clubs isn't exactly right, what is?* I continued journaling for answers. Creative work that made me feel this alive was now essential. To spend maximum time with my girls, I wanted to do this work mostly from home.

What if I could share the spiritual truths I was learning with others? What if I could teach in my living room and coach people in my own home office? A new possibility began to burn in my heart.

"Who are *you* to teach this stuff? You're hardly an expert on spiritual growth." The inner critic, an aspect of the scared ego, spoke up once again. On and on it went, giving me all kinds of reasons I wasn't qualified to follow this new spark of joyful possibility. Despite my ego's pushback, again I felt exhilaration combined with fear, a sign I was on track.

A serendipitous meeting led me to a luscious gift of an experience I couldn't have conceived in my mind, let alone consciously sought out. A few days post 9-11, my daughter and I were volunteering in an art-making humanitarian community project to help raise relief funds. "I don't usually approach people like this, but something tells me you might enjoy this." A magical-looking woman with sparkly cat eyes, Kate Thompson, admired my art and handed me a juicy, colorful brochure that spoke my language.

We didn't have the money, but I couldn't stop looking at the brochure. One month later I said yes anyway and gleefully joined the year-long training in Expressive Arts Therapy (EAT).

We were thirteen women, sharing our fears and dreams in a circle and learning tools for healing and manifesting our hearts' desires. Two months into the training, I began teaching my first class, *Reconnecting with your Spirit*, out of my living room. Six other mothers and I convened to connect with our truth and support one another in excavating what was "missing" from our apparently ideal lives.

And then one day, I woke up crying for no apparent reason. I spent that entire summer wiping away tears that had no known source. I realize now that I was grieving. About what, I didn't then know.

Around this same time, I sought massage therapy treatment for chronic shoulder pain. The pain felt like a bullet lodged in my left shoulder blade. After the second visit to the massage therapist, I walked back to my car, put the key in the ignition, and paused. A palpable sensation stopped me from turning the key. If I could translate the feeling I would describe it as a longing—a longing for more: more love, more joy, more fullness of life. Oddly and disturbingly, however, this powerful emotion and physical sensation showed up not in my heart, but as a deep pang in my womb. My pelvis and hips—the body's center of creativity—seemed to be crying out for attention. A hunger pang of the spirit, perhaps.

It was as though my body was saying, "There's a yearning in here that you have never acknowledged. Hear me now!" This yearning that was now pulsating throughout my entire body.

Maybe because the massage seemed to bring on this strange and moving occurrence, I began developing a crush on the massage therapist. One day, my husband told me that for days I'd been calling out a man's name in my sleep. It was the name of the therapist. I was shocked. I felt deeply saddened and horribly guilty for unconsciously causing my husband such terrible pain. I stopped seeing the therapist for massage, and my husband and I began couple's counseling.

Meanwhile, I was becoming more awakened to long-buried heart's desires. Each week, I would lead my *Reconnecting with Your Spirit* participants in guided meditations to connect with their own wise knowing of what was calling them. For all of us, new inspirations and possibilities began to surface. Inner dreams, nighttime dreams, and new life dreams came to the fore. As I connected more and more with my soul during journaling and meditation, the restlessness, uncertainty, and angst I initially felt around my career began to transform into desire.

Over and over, I received the same message:

> We are not here solely to raise families, earn a living, and
> eventually retire in comfort to *someday* live our *real* dreams.

Now I saw that we each carry unique gifts and talents—our individual, shining contributions to humanity. And when we say yes, we light up the world and make it a better place for all of us. Our purpose is to express and share these gifts in everything we do, including our relationships, parenting, and work. When we're living our purpose, it infuses all that we do with meaning and aliveness.

This message spoke to me so powerfully that I felt as though I'd broken through to the deeper truth of life. Each moment began to take on this greater meaning. I began to feel an intense and beautiful awakening about why I was here. *This was the something missing.* Before this time, the concept that we have a purpose beyond our everyday work and parenting had never even occurred to me. I began to feel a burning desire—almost a sense of urgency—to know and share my gifts, to help others in meaningful ways, to open to a new adventure.

The old me was falling away. I was questioning everything about my outer existence. I was in love with the custom home that I had put my heart and creativity into designing. But I began to question the need for a big house that was draining our bank account and leaving no room for fun, much less travel or adventure. Even more painful, it was dawning on me that my marriage was in serious trouble.

The intimacy I was beginning to have with my own soul ignited a deep desire to feel an emotional connection with my husband—something I could now see clearly was sadly lacking. Unresolved conflict and our shifting values had created a stark void. I felt terribly lonely in the relationship. We had grown worlds apart.

Add to this that I had also made room to hear the call of my soul, which was adding a whole other rich and exciting dimension to my life. My inner world had come alive with possibility.

An aching shoulder took me to the massage therapist, which catalyzed me into seeing where I had fallen asleep to my own expansion—to the truth of who I really was as a spiritual being. I realized that I couldn't go back to my former self. I had heard the call. I had to learn and grow and live out a unique destiny. My soul was nudging me to strike out and take a chance, to do something that would contribute to the healing of our planet. It was time to move forward with the next chapter of my life.

It felt like the brilliant sun breaking through after years of monotone gray skies. A new enthusiasm revitalized my zest for life. I wanted nothing more than to create this next chapter with my husband. I had read about couples who take their kids out of school to learn at sea while sailing around the world. Or people who travel to a third-world country to help others by participating in a humanitarian project. It thrilled me to think about the possibilities. Yes, it would be a big shift and we would have a lot of details to figure out, but we'd built a house and made other life-changing moves together. I knew that if we were both on board, we could make it happen.

I sensed that if we joined together to create something bigger than ourselves, as a purposeful contribution to humanity, it would bring us closer than ever before. We'd have a chance for a fresh start. I also felt, deep down, that if we did not consciously embark on *something* new together, our marriage would not make it.

We had over a year of couple's therapy, and very little changed.

I consulted with an intuitive counselor, Gail Ferguson, who came highly recommended. Gail is a well-respected, internationally renowned author and speaker on awakening intuition. A formidable woman in her seventies, she was well aware of the gravity of my situation. I told her I had two beautiful daughters and a picture-perfect life that I had worked hard to create. My husband was a good provider. We had been together for twenty-two years. No reasonable (read: sane) person throws that away. The thought of divorce was unthinkable to me. I always believed that if two devoted people worked hard enough at their marriage, they could get through anything.

Gail said frankly, "Your spirit desperately needs adventure and new experiences to grow. You are suffocating." Then she added, "The problem is, your husband is happy with the way things are. You have come to a turning point—a crossroads. Your values are no longer the same. You now each want very different things from life." With tactful grace, she concluded, "Your marriage died a long time ago."

On my way home, the words *you are suffocating* resounded over and over in my awareness. In fact, I could not drive more than a mile before I had to pull over and get my bearings. I made it into the nearest Starbucks, and felt the entire coffee shop fill up with the shocking sense of *oh-my-God-is-my-life-as-I've-always-dreamed-it-really-ending-this-abruptly?* I hadn't experienced this feeling since my father died at the age of forty-nine from a sudden heart attack, when I was just sixteen years old. Gail's assessment broke through my denial. *You are suffocating.* Her confirmation of my deeper knowing spoke to me once more: *your marriage is over.*

How could I say yes to acting on this—to what felt like a life-shattering revelation? My ego continued to resist the prospect of divorce, of our sweet family divided into two separate households and futures. Married for over two decades. Overall it was a good enough life, wasn't it? Was I even right to expect more? To desire more? Even if my spirit *was* suffocating, how could I burst the bubble of my daughters' dream of being raised by their two beloved parents in the beautiful home that I had invested so much of my heart in creating?

Couldn't we just get by, at least until my daughters were independent and on their own?

Making a choice that would hurt my children was agonizing. To ease the pain, I, of course, hoped that my husband would at least reach the same understanding about our marriage that I had so that we could make a peaceful transition together. That didn't happen. The realization on his part did come, but not until much later.

Add to this that my work as a spiritual teacher was only in the embryo stage. Since leaving the law, I had spent years raising my children and tending to non-income-producing pursuits, like running our household, designing our home, and volunteering in my kids' schools. I had virtually no income of my own.

I was afraid I wouldn't be able to support myself and my daughters financially, that I was crazy for letting go of my security, and that I had a good enough life and I was being foolish to take such a huge risk and let it all go. The critical voice within me said I was "a dreamer" and I should "get real." "You don't always get what you want," it went on.

Although I had done all I could to revive our marriage and make it work to the best of my ability, I was still unwilling to accept what felt like defeat. Not succeeding made me feel selfish and guilty. Why couldn't I find a way to feel the love I had felt with him during our courtship? Since he seemed happy with the way things were, I worried that there was something fundamentally *wrong* with me for not being able to change the way I felt. The voice of fear made me feel confused, saying that I was misinformed and making a big mistake.

To get clarity, I would journal my thoughts and feelings. Dumping my fears on the page helped immensely. I would write until I felt a release.

I'm afraid of making a mistake.

I'm afraid of being broke.

I'm afraid I'll never find the heart-connected relationship my heart so longs for.

In contrast to the voice of doubt, worry, and fear, another voice came through my journaling that was comforting and wise: the voice of my soul, which I call *Spirit*.

Dear Spirit, Please talk to me. Please tell me what I should do.

I would intentionally connect with this inner wise guide, asking for encouragement and advice. I continued this for months, journaling and journaling, asking for insight and advice from Spirit. A pattern began to emerge. I kept hearing Spirit say:

It's time to fly free now.

Go.

New opportunities await.

You are safe.

It's time to soar.

This uplifting guidance was the voice of freedom—of a whole new possibility. Whenever I heard it, my entire body took a deep exhale, allowing excitement for a new life chapter to enter. It was as if the wisdom of my body knew something that I did not.

I realized that I had this choice: stay married and live a lie, or say yes to a new life, knowing it would mean letting go of my outer security and the dream of my life as I had envisioned it. The dream of creating a loving partnership with the father of my children. A partnership in which we would support each other's passions, explore the world together, and model for our daughters the values of deep caring, mutual admiration, and respect.

The truth is, our daughters weren't seeing their parents loving each other in this way. As much as I wanted to avoid the pain of divorce for all of us, I knew that they deserved a truer model of love.

I cannot tell you how many countless hours I spent scouring local Seattle bookstores in search of a story like mine. Surely I was not the only woman on the planet whose life outwardly appeared picture-perfect but who now felt like nothing in her existence fit who she had become. I read literally hundreds of books on transition, divorce, and change, hoping to find a trace of evidence that I was not crazy, selfish, mean, or stupid. That I was not forever sentenced to doing what seemed like the right thing, rather than the right thing *for me*.

Life as I knew it ended the day I rented a house and moved out of our family home. I left behind everything I had ever received approval for.

I did not know where I was headed. I only knew that I had to stay true to myself. To stay true to myself meant listening to my inner wise voice. Once I heard what this voice was telling me, staying in the marriage no longer felt like a choice. I was being called to acknowledge this ending and move forward.

I said yes to my inner direction and stepped into a new world.

Anchoring in Spirit

I began a new life as a single person. Single was not an identity I was familiar with. For more than two decades, I had seen myself as married. I was half of a couple. I had my life figured out. I did not know how to be single, nor did I want to live without my two daughters half of the time. *They were my world.* All of a sudden, I had an instant empty nest when they were with their dad, and I missed them terribly.

I remember one Friday evening, around 10 p.m., feeling isolated and alone in my charming old craftsman rental house, thirty minutes from our family home. I'd said yes to caring for this great transition house while the owners took a sabbatical in Australia for a year. I'd been intentionally visualizing a home by the water and checking rental listings often. Spirit, again, was handing me a gem. With a backyard Zen garden, two extra rooms for my girls, and a big room upstairs for teaching my classes, the house was perfect. And it was only a five-minute walk to the healing oasis of beautiful Green Lake.

Still, I was like a cedar tree that had been uprooted. This didn't feel like my house. I hadn't yet sunk my roots deep enough into my new life—or my new emerging self— to feel stable and secure.

To say I felt wobbly was an understatement.

"If I died tonight, no one would know." Here I was, in my three-bedroom "single" house on a Friday night, feeling displaced, thinking this somewhat morbid but very real thought. "Hmmm … I wonder how long it would take for someone to find me?" I mused, a bit of humor creeping in.

Fortunately I had the wherewithal to email my sadness to my Expressive Arts Therapy (EAT) training group, asking them for support in navigating this new territory. Within an hour, a couple of reassuring emails arrived. My loving colleagues let me know that I was not alone—they were sending me love and holding me in their thoughts.

What gave me day-to-day, or I should say more accurately moment-to-moment, courage to make this change was my connection to Spirit. I experience Spirit as the channel through which my soul speaks to me. It may be even larger than my soul, such as the Universal intelligence, Great Creator, God, or the Divine. I am not concerned with delineating the fullness of this source. I only know that Spirit connects me with the very personal and loving essence of what I feel as my higher self and soul.

From the moment I realized our marriage had died, I began relying daily on Spirit's wise guidance as my anchor in what felt like swimming alone in a vast ocean out of view of any shore.

I kept a journal on my laptop, writing to Spirit daily, asking for answers, advice, comfort, and solutions whenever I felt fear or doubt. For example, one of my journal entries reads:

Dear Spirit,

I really want to feel free. I know I need projects to sink my life into. I feel hopeless in some ways. I wonder in this moment if I should go back to my marriage … although, no, we can't make our marriage work, we've already tried that. I can't even open up to him in my so vulnerable way, and I don't know why. I don't know why. I don't know why.

I have always been successful, so why does this seem to be harder now? Too much time on my hands? In a rut? I don't know. But I am tired of looking for ways out of it. All the times I made positive change work in my life I had some structure I was going to. College, Boston with John, law school, Seattle with John, building the house, the different jobs I had. Always a structure. I just need to pray and pray for the new structure, because God! … I am so ready. I am so ready. I am so ready.

Love,
Betsy

And Spirit answered:

Dearest Betsy,

You know how much I adore you. You are the light of my life. Nothing you can do is wrong. Here's the thing: You are free! You made a bold move to follow your inner guidance, and you are so supported! You are a spiritual warrior of the highest proportions. Never underestimate the power of your spirit to move you forward. Now hear this: there is absolutely nothing you cannot create. You are simply in an in-between time right now. Let yourself grieve. The new structure you desire is coming. Offer another workshop! Surround yourself with like-minded people who will lift you as you lift them. Know that you are never alone. Never alone. I am always here for you. You rock!

Love,
Spirit

Spirit reminded me of the truth. At the same time that I was experiencing the exhilaration of this new beginning, I was also grieving the end of the dream and vision for my life as I had conceived it. With this wise guide by my side, I felt loved and supported in ways that my well-meaning friends and family were not able to express. Alongside moments of grief, I began to experience life on a whole new level, feeling a wonderful, new sense of freedom. Freedom to be who I *really* was—outside of my role as wife and caretaker of a traditional family unit.

I had many moments of doubt where I questioned letting go of my old life. When this happened, Spirit would intervene again and comfort me, reminding me that I was on my path, following the directive of my soul.

I now have a full-time coaching, teaching, and writing career. I am incredibly grateful to be living my passionate life purpose. I know deep in my bones what I am here for, and I have the blessed honor of partnering with beloved clients like you, people who are courageously searching and excavating their hearts for answers to their most pressing and profound life questions. This is work that nourishes my soul each and every day.

Cultivating a Partnership with Your Soul

It is my joy to help you cultivate this same intimate partnership with your inner wise guidance. This wise part of you goes by many names. Psychological, holistic healing, and spiritual traditions variously refer to inner guidance as intuition, the higher self, your spirit, the soul, or true self, which are terms I use variably in this book. If the term soul carries a religious connotation that feels oppressive to you or you simply cannot relate to it, choose a name that feels right for you. You can even call it your Muse, Creative Catalyst, Fairy Godmother or Wise Wizard.

To begin to connect with the love, comfort, and guidance your soul desires to give, you only need to say yes. As my beloved teacher Denise Linn says, "Where intention goes, energy flows." Your sincere intention is a powerful catalyst. An affirmation such as, *I am ready to create a deeply rewarding partnership with my soul,* will jumpstart your lifeline to Spirit.

Like any relationship, your bond with your soul thrives on communication. The first step is asking for what you desire and requesting that your wise guide show you the way. The second part is opening yourself to receive answers to your communications.

For me, spending time communing with my soul has been incredibly enriching. It is a bond that will bring more joy, depth, and intimacy to your life than you have imagined. The sweetness of your intimacy with your soul will ripple out and expand, strengthen and enliven every aspect of your life and relationships.

Connecting with your inner wise guidance is a foundational practice that will strengthen your trust in yourself to make clear choices, even when life feels wobbly and uncertain. It will also increase your sense of safety and well-being as you enter the new territory of what's next. When you begin to trust what you sense or hear, you will feel stronger, more confident, and more at peace with moving forward on your soul's inner nudges.

This trust is your ticket to freeing yourself to follow your heart.

I invite you in this moment to take a deep breath and relax. Say yes to receiving the messages of your soul. This does not mean that you have to act immediately on any guidance you sense. You have free will—you are in charge of when and how you want to move forward on any direction you get.

Sometimes my clients will resist hearing their own wise guidance because they fear the changes it might bring to their lives. This fear is natural. It helps to remember that you are in charge. I encourage you to simply become informed. Self-knowledge is always empowering. Give yourself permission to begin by connecting to your heart and witnessing how it is speaking to you. You can decide which actions you would like to take later, if you choose.

In my workshops, participants often ask: How can I tell if I am connecting with my true source of wisdom? You will know by how you feel. Your inner wise guidance has a much different *feeling tone* from the voice of the ego or the voice of fear. True guidance feels comforting, caring, and unconditionally loving. This wisdom will feel right in your gut and put you at ease. Wise guidance is the voice of love.

Exercise: *Partner with Your Soul*

Many a lover has found sustenance and solace in writing to a sweetheart. I have journaled since I was child, but my writing shifted when my marriage dissolved. I needed solid anchoring from a new source. A deeper reservoir of intelligence. A spiritual rock that I could count on in the middle of the night and in my darkest moments of sadness, anger, or despair.

As you connect with your soul, feel free to share your feelings and thoughts. Nothing is off limits—you are writing to your truest confidante. A good way to begin is simply to ask for what you desire. For example, if you want comfort, you can ask for that. If you need clarity, request clear knowing.

I listen to what I hear back, and take dictation. I don't hear a human voice. Rather, I *sense* the words. You also may get a feeling or *sense* of what your guidance is telling you. The key is using your imagination, a core channel our inner wisdom uses to reach us. If you imagine that your wise self is speaking to you, you *will* get an answer.

This is a practice. You are honing your intuitive gift as you go. When I lead workshop participants in this exercise, people invariably receive exactly what they need in order to feel better.

Here's an example:

> *Dear Spirit,*
>
> *I am feeling so frustrated about my life. I wish this would all go away. This is so much harder than I thought it would be! I feel so uncertain right now. Please comfort me. Please show me my next step.*
>
> *Love,*
> *Betsy*

Now you:

Dear _____,

Love,

Now write a note from this wise, loving guide back to yourself.

For me, Spirit sometimes comes through as a single being, or often as a team of spiritual advisors. Yours may be different. Just trust what comes. Again, it can be any length. Just write until you feel complete. For example:

Dearest Beloved of our Heart,

We want you to know how much we adore you. Nothing you could ever do or say could change our deep love for you. Every time we see and hear you, we light up. We are just plain enamored with you, Beloved! Now hear this, you are feeling frustrated right now because, yes, it feels hard. We get it, we do. But we want you to know that you are on track, even when you don't feel that you are, you are. You are doing amazing things, beloved. You just forget! We want you to write down all the goodness in your life. Then you will feel better. This is your next step—write down what is working. Start with the tiniest thing. And remember that we love you—forever and always!

Love,
Spirit

Your turn:

Dear _____,

Love,

Are You Ready to Become Real?

It is often challenging to wrap our minds around this, but the truth is that we are so much more powerful than we know. We are divinely guided co-creators of our lives. We are here to grow and expand and become more than we ever thought possible. We are spiritual beings having a human experience.

> *The true purpose of your life is to wake up to, and follow, your own unique destiny.*

To wake up to this truth and know it in every cell, tissue, and bone in your body is a life-changing transformation—a path I have been on since I heeded Spirit's completely nonsensical guidance to get on stage and attempt to make people laugh. I am passionate about transformation because it is tantamount to discovering the secret of life, over and over, as we dance into finer and truer expressions of our authentic selves. It is what author Margery Williams refers to in the story of *The Velveteen Rabbit* as *becoming real*.

There is a wise part of you, your soul, that already has this awareness. You are ready for more—to know and *become real*—to step more fully into your true, authentic self. To say yes to your destiny as you free yourself to follow your heart. I offer myself as your guide. We are on this journey together. In the pages of this book, I will take you every step of the way, as I do my private coaching clients.

The only thing this process of becoming real asks is that you stay open. To be willing to see your situation and your life through a fresh lens of possibility. Profound realizations come by seeing with *real eyes*, which is tantamount to seeing with new eyes. Seeing with new eyes brings you into a whole new perception of what is possible for you and your life.

I encourage you to see the journey you are about to embark on as a new adventure—an adventure unlike any you have ever taken before. It is, as Joseph Campbell calls it, a hero's journey. You are the brilliant hero of your own life, and this is the first day of a brand new chapter that is unfolding as you read these words. Know that you are safe.

In addition to having me as your guide, you are being ushered along and anchored by your own inner wise guidance—the guidance that led you to pick up this book. You are well supported. So take a breath, relax, and feel this support in your body. You are well on your way to discovering the blueprint of your soul's destiny.

2

 Turning to Gold

There is something in every one of you that waits and listens for the sound of the genuine in yourself. It is the only true guide you will ever have. And if you cannot hear it, you will all of your life spend your days on the ends of strings that somebody else pulls.

~ Howard Thurman

Love happens every moment
Stay tuned to love
Give up everything you are clinging to
Stay tuned to what's calling
A more grand and glorious you is emerging
Let the doors fling wide open
For you, my love
For you … are a dream come true

~ A Journal Entry

Imagine that. *You* are a dream come true. You came here with a dream, a vision, for your life. A dream to express, contribute, and experience your true nature, all of which flow from your unique destiny. You hold your destiny within you like a spark in your heart that yearns to catch fire.

Since you were *born* with the blueprint or map of your destiny wired into your cellular make up—your DNA—it is not something you have to *figure out*. Rather, you simply become more and more *available* to it as your awareness of who you really are expands, one clue or inspiration—one soul nudge—at a time. The more you say yes to, and act on, what your heart is guiding you to do and be, the more you see and experience your destiny unfold. And the more you find yourself living it.

As you work with the tools and do the exercises in these pages, you will find yourself waking up and coming more alive to your true nature. You will receive guidance from your intuition or soul and begin to take small steps in the direction you are being led. The work itself will become your magic wand, taking you through an alchemical process, as you turn your own inner dross into gold.

I remember a session I had years ago with a wise and lovely spiritual counselor, Jan Santora. I must have been stressing about how much time the process of change was taking—about how much work it was to journal, meditate, and fit in all the things I was doing to find clarity. I told her I did not have time for "all this inner work." I needed to get to work (as in, find a paying job) and make money. Jan replied, "Betsy, this *is* the work."

I understand now what I did not get then. We create our lives from the *inside* out. Everything you experience in your life, including the paying dream job, is simply a reflection of your *inner* landscape. As you do your self-discovery, reflection, and healing, you transform inside, and the circumstances and situations of your outer life begin to take on new aliveness and color as well.

It is common to experience transformation as one step forward, two steps back. When you feel tired, rest. If you need a break, take one.

Remember that you are turning to gold, and this has a divine
timing of its own.

Be Gentle With Yourself

As you do the exercises, you may find yourself having a whole range of emotions, from profound joy to deep grief. Know that this is part of the process and is nothing to fear. Your emotions are not who you are. As my mentor, Dr. Darren Weissman, says, e-motions are simply "energy in motion."

I like to think about emotions as clouds—sometimes storm clouds—that come and go. Our emotional weather may move through like a hurricane, a light shower, or a long spell of sunny, warm days. As energy in motion, emotions only ask to be felt and released. Feeling is healing. If you are concerned or fearful of getting lost in an emotion, give yourself a daily time limit, such as thirty minutes, to meet the emotion, feel its sensation in your body, and release what's coming up.

I encourage you to be gentle with yourself in this process of freeing yourself to follow your heart. When you feel resistance to anything going on in your life, this is an invitation to pause and breathe. Your breath is miraculous. Taking in a few full, deep breaths moves the stuck energy through the body. Breathing helps to slow repetitive thoughts that make you feel tense at best and crazy at worst—the mind chatter that goes round and round speaking the same unproductive and often critical loop.

Breathing begins to relax you. Relaxing helps you connect to your body's wisdom. As you breathe and relax, you more easily tune in to your emotions and allow them to freely move through you.

Have compassion for inner weather moving through you. You are not your situation or your circumstances. If you hyphenate the word *compassion* it becomes *come-pass-on*. Imagine how much lighter we would all feel if we remembered to invite feelings of anger, sadness, and betrayal to simply *come-pass-on*. Be as compassionate with your self as you would be with a small child experiencing sadness, anger, or grief.

I love the wisdom of this quote by Geneen Roth: "All any feeling wants is to be welcomed with tenderness."[2] This is all any feeling wants. To be welcomed, accepted, and acknowledged. *With love and tenderness.*

Whatever you are navigating in your life, however painful, is part of your unfolding destiny. Although you may not see it now, your pain is a huge gift, in that healing through it brings you closer to wholeness and bliss. As you release energy through tears or a run, for example, you are cleansing and clearing space for your dreams. Meeting and releasing your emotions is your bridge to freedom, bringing you closer to your heart's desires.

Exercise: *Checking in with Your Heart*

We each have an inner tender self, like a small, sweet child, who needs love and attention on a regular basis—often, several times a day. Especially in times of change, transition, or crisis, your prominent emotion may be the feeling of *unsafe*. What if each time you felt off balance you stopped, checked in with this inner tender being, and asked, "How are you feeling? What do you need right now?"

Try this:

> Pause.
>
> Breathe in and out through your nose. Take in a few nice deep breaths.
>
> Put one hand on your heart and one hand on your belly, and ask:
>
> What is the emotion I am feeling right now?
>
> Name the emotion and breathe into it. Continue to breathe until you feel a release or lightening of your energy.
>
> Now ask yourself: What do I need right now?

Seeing Yourself with New Eyes

Before my move to the Green Lake house, when I began to feel my marriage unravel, it felt as though an earthquake had shaken the very foundation of my existence. I was terribly confused about what was happening. The crux of my constant questioning was, "Should I stay or should I go?" Long before I was ready to make such a life-altering decision, I believed I *should* already have an answer. I felt tremendous pressure to know what was next for me and my family.

Not surprisingly, I felt this same pressure when I was searching for my passionate new career. The ego so fears uncertainty that it pushes us to *know*—to have clarity before the soul is ready to deliver it.

Without consciously realizing it, I began to soothe my worried mind with daily walks to our neighborhood cemetery set high on a manicured, grassy hill. Backed by a forest of cedar and fir trees, where the sun poured through and lit up the rolling terrain on a pristine morning, this was a particularly beautiful part of our semirural community. I would walk up the winding road to the hilltop and wrap my arms around the twin-trunked, majestic, old cedar tree that anchored the landscape. In my imagination, *my tree*, as I came to call it, represented the fulfilled love relationship I so longed for with a mate.

In native traditions, trees are believed to have their own spirit. Befriending a special tree can bring immense healing to the individual seeking comfort and guidance. It's as if the tree transfers its thriving earth energy to those who ask for it and open to receive it.

My sojourns to the cemetery on the hill became both a comforting and grounding ritual. This was a place I could go to be with my uncertainty. My tree was a powerful anchor for my spirit. I poured out my heart, sharing my worries, concerns, fears, and greatest hopes. During these walks, I learned to let go and allow myself to *not* know. I let myself just be with what was.

My tree, in turn, offered me its strength and unconditional love. What I didn't see then is that my former identity as a devoted wife and at-home mom was dissolving to make room for a new identity. This new identity was off in the mysterious future, but thanks to the visits to my tree, I had space to grieve even before I knew what was leaving.

Around this time, one of my spiritual teachers, author Sonia Choquette, suggested that I "name my spirit." As I saw it, she was encouraging me to connect with the voice of my soul—my spiritual self. Sonia seemed to sense that for years I had been denying a part of my true expression. Working hard to "make it" as an attorney had sent my playful, artist self underground. At the very least, I had not been acknowledging or affirming my spirit's unique gifts and beauty. Naming my spirit would be a powerful act of reclaiming the parts of myself I had buried in my quest to be a dutiful lawyer, wife, and mother.

The question was, what had I buried? What was I not seeing that was an important aspect of my true essence? I thought about the quality I would need to possess if my marriage did not make it. The answer that came was *courage*.

I named my spirit *Braveheart Beauty*. *Braveheart* represented the courage to follow my heart's guidance, no matter how unpopular my decision. *Beauty* symbolized my love for aesthetic beauty and my desire to affirm both my inner and outer beauty. I liked the way it sounded. Voicing it made my heart sing. My spirit name felt like a bold declaration of who I was becoming.

Part of my daily ritual, while communing with my tree, was writing my spirit name with a stick in the earth. I would sit with my spine against my twin tree's wide trunk, close my eyes and breathe, and listen for any messages it had to give me. I could feel its vibrant energy move up the base of my spine to the top of my head, both energizing and infusing me with a feeling of deep peace.

In the curved opening where the single trunk divided into two, I would leave small gifts of gratitude. One day, I arrived to find a delightful surprise in the same place I placed my flower offerings. A three-inch plastic, red Santa Claus smiled back at me. I took this as a very good sign. For me, Santa represented gifts, abundance, and thriving. With this little treasure, I heard divine direction saying, "Ho, ho, ho, no matter what happens, you are gifted. The Universe is abundant—you live in an infinitely giving and nourishing place. You will be amply supported."

 Exercise: *Name Your Spirit*

Now you:

I invite you to name your Spirit.

To name your spirit helps you loosen your grip on the identity of your personality and the roles you have taken on in your everyday life. When you begin instead to identify with your soul, you are freed from having to show up in ways that no longer fit who you have become. At your core, you are a spiritual being here to fulfill a purpose and destiny. As much as you may want to keep your life as you know it the same, sometimes your destiny is calling you to new horizons.

Whether you simply want to become more your true self, or it feels like a tsunami is threatening to wash away something you've come to rely on, you need an enduring, reliable anchor to hold you steady and make you feel safe. This anchor is your soul, always guiding you to a safe shore.

Sometimes your spirit name comes when you relax, breathe, and get quiet.

I invite you to go inside, connect to your heart, and ask, "What is my spirit name?"

Or you can connect to your spirit and ask *it* to name *you*.

Write down what comes, even if you don't get a direct or clear response. A few minutes of writing might bring forth your name. If not, the following prompts may reveal a name. Know that your spirit name isn't etched in stone—it's *your* name—you can always change it if you choose.

- One quality I love about my spirit is …

- One thing that others sometimes don't acknowledge about me is …

- Weaving these qualities into my spirit name, I might call myself …

- A wise part of you always knows your answer. Ask yourself, If I *knew* my spirit name, it would be …

Living True to Yourself

We are born into life as brand new babies, free of the expectations of others. As souls coming to "earth school" to live this dream, we wait at the door of this incarnation with a burning desire to bring our dream into reality. We are full of joy and unbridled enthusiasm, knowing that we are the co-creators of our own experience. So many possibilities—so much ahead!

We arrive with an innate knowing that no one else can live our exquisite destiny, nor can we live anyone else's. We know that we are bringing gifts, talents, dreams, and potential yearning to be actualized. We understand that becoming more real will grow and expand us. That we will feel more and more alive.

And then we are conditioned by the rules and indoctrination of well-meaning parents, relatives, teachers, media, and society. We are showered with input from others as they give us *their own ideas* of who we are and who we should be.

And we forget.

We forget that we are much more than the roles we play or the labels we use to define ourselves. Roles like mother, father, child, sister, brother, co-worker, spouse, or CEO of the company. We forget that these roles and labels allow us to be in service to our spiritual unfolding, but they are not the goal of life in and of themselves. In short, we forget the bigger purpose of what we came here to do.

We do our best to fit in, belong, and do the right things in order to be loved and feel secure. At some point, we wake up to the truth, as Bronnie Ware's patients did toward the end of their lives, that we've been working very hard to make everyone happy except ourselves. We discover that living the life *others* expect of us can never bring true fulfillment.

For example, I remember when I first began asking the question, *If not law, what is my passion?* At the time my daughters were ages six and nine. I had left my law job. I now had some time to attend to my burning desire to explore my passion and true purpose. I used this time for soul-searching whenever I could, which never seemed to be often enough. Even though I was temporarily "unemployed," my daughters' needs, household chores, and volunteer commitments always seemed to claim my time and get most of my attention.

Add to this that I often took care of my niece after school while my sister worked. As much as I adored her, as did my girls, I began to feel resentful of my sister for not reciprocating the childcare I was providing. Secretly I was seething inside because she was not offering to have *my kids* over to play at her house so that I could have some quiet time for my own creative work. I had brought it up with her, but because she was invariably tired or stressed after work, she declined. One day, I took a seemingly small step that ended up rippling out into the rest of my life.

I wrote my sister a letter admitting that I had been feeling resentful for some time. I shared that I had been expecting her to do something that she was clearly unwilling to do, and that I was now letting go of my own unfulfilled expectations. I also wrote that I would no longer expect myself to care for her daughter if it meant not meeting my own needs for time alone to do my work. I promised her (and myself) that I would not be angry or resentful any longer. I was ready to let it all go.

I had no idea *how* I would get more time for myself, but the act of writing this letter took a huge weight off my shoulders. Simply by revealing my truth to my sister in a calm and non-blaming way, I felt a great sense of relief. With this one action, I was declaring to the Universe, "Okay, I'm ready to live *my* life now!" Shortly after this, I had my stand-up comedy dream and was launched into a brand-new, life-changing adventure.

Looking back, I see that I had made an authentically powerful decision. Not only did I set a clear boundary with my sister, I made a decision to view myself differently. I chose to stop identifying solely with my role as a nurturing caretaker. I began to see myself not as a *role* but as a *soul*—a soul whose purpose was to find my passion and live my full potential. In a world that generally only recognizes paid work as *real* work, I dared to make my creative unfolding *my work*.

Making Space for Your Dream

In our work together, my coaching clients often discover that they, too, have been doing things out of a sense of duty or obligation—activities that don't turn them on or that just leave them feeling burdened or resentful. They have full schedules, and they don't see how to fit in time to care for themselves, much less find their passion or hear the call of their soul.

I invite my clients to fly above their lives and see from a new vantage point. What have they been saying yes to that they really don't enjoy? What is draining their energy—both at home and at work? Energy drains may take the form of people, situations, or tasks. What feels heavy, sad, or just plain annoying? Often one person, circumstance, or task rises to the surface above the rest.

For example, one of my clients, Jennifer, wanted to let go of volunteering on a church committee. After reflecting further, she realized that she no longer resonated with her church's philosophy—she wanted to stop attending altogether. Jennifer had felt this way for some time, but feared disappointing the church leadership and fellow congregants. We talked about it and after voicing her fears, she became clear that by being honest with herself and others, she could still keep the relationships that mattered most to her. She left my office feeling more free—and excited to explore potential new places of worship with her partner.

The following exercise will help you identify the things, people, or tasks that are siphoning off your precious life energy. The more drains you can eliminate, delegate, or simply release, the more energy you will have available to you to feed what truly matters to you—including your dreams. Identifying your energy drains and taking one small step is an act of authentic power. Take one step forward, and the Universe will meet you halfway.

 Exercise: *Speaking Your Truth ~ An Act of Power*

I invite you to let the answers to the following questions come to you in a stream of consciousness. In other words, try not to "think them up." When you're thinking, your intellect gets in the way of your wise body's knowing. To connect with your inner wisdom, put one hand on your belly and the other on your heart. Take a few deep breaths and continue until you feel quiet and still. Then listen to your heart's responses to the questions and jot down what you hear.

- If I am really honest with myself, I no longer want to …

- I'm actually sick and tired of …

- It's time for me to let go of …

Look over your responses. Choose one thing you would like to release. If you feel resistant to letting it go, list your fears until you've dumped them all on the page:

- When I imagine letting go of _____, I'm afraid of …

- I'm afraid of …

- I'm afraid of …

- Now fill in this blank: Regarding letting go of _____, my wise guidance says …

Taking a step is an act of power. It affirms your spirit and strengthens your resolve to make the next move. What one small step could you take to move forward? Writing it down makes it more likely you'll do it.

The one small step I will take is …

Choosing a New Identity

I have a dear friend who I am proud to call my soul sister. Since becoming close friends in junior high school, we have shared tremendous joys and sheltered each other from the storms of life. Recently, Marianne called me to say that her beloved position teaching kindergarten had been reassigned to a new teacher with much less experience. Marianne was used to putting in long hours on a daily basis to bring her all to her students and her craft. She loved her kindergarten job, and was well liked by peers, administrators, students, and parents. She always received shining reviews from her principal and was offered travel and other professional development and leadership opportunities.

However, because of an administrative glitch in communication early on in her teaching career, something happened midstream that shook her to the core. After twelve years as a successful teacher, she was mandated by the state to go back and earn an additional master's degree in order to keep her teaching job. She dutifully completed the degree, and then the bottom fell out of her world. Her kindergarten position had been filled. She was offered a position teaching another grade, but teaching five- and six-year-olds was her true love and passion. And no other kindergarten jobs were showing up.

She was both angry and sad and still a bit in shock that her principal had filled her position. "I realize my *entire identity* is tied up in being a kindergarten teacher," she said. "Look at me, I am exhausted, I am grieving, and I get up every morning and start applying for teaching jobs I don't even want! I see that I'm only doing this so I don't have to loosen my grip on my identity as a kindergarten teacher."

"I have always been a hard worker," she added. "I've always gone the extra mile. Well, I've learned one thing: that you will always be rewarded for working hard is not true. There is no guarantee that hard work will bring you the rewards you seek."

Of course I felt her deep pain and have tremendous compassion for Marianne. Needless to say, I would never have wished upon her the loss of her dream job. But since she finds herself in this situation and is unable to go back in time, I see an opportunity for her to grieve this ending, discover what else her heart desires, and reclaim her happiness.

I've seen Marianne create gorgeous paintings, sculpt clay into exquisite, lifelike forms, speak as a visionary leader on topics of cross-cultural education, and more.

She has led groups internationally and traveled the globe. I can easily see that if this door is closing, the Universe and her soul are calling her into service in other exciting and expansive ways. The world is absolutely her oyster.

Marianne's path may very well lead her back to teaching kindergarten. The delay can only be temporary if this is her soul's ultimate desire. In the meantime, the Universe is nudging her to have, do, or be something that will no doubt illuminate her life. Her own recognition of being attached to her identity as a kindergarten teacher is hugely freeing in and of itself.

The same is true for you. Even in the midst of painful loss, the truth is that anything going away or shifting in your life is making room for a new, more glorious you to emerge. You live in a loving, purposeful Universe that has your back. Divine order is orchestrating a plan that you simply cannot see when you are attached to life staying the same.

The key is shifting your gaze away from the rubble of your loss. Until you turn toward the light shining through the door that is waiting for you to walk through, you may as well be blind. The bright new beginnings remain completely hidden from view. The good news is that endings only come about because something new—and more right for you—is *calling*.

The question is, *what* is calling? And how do you find it?

How do you shift your focus away from the scattered pieces of your former dream and toward this sometimes elusive *something new*?

When you become separated from your career or relationship identity, whether the separation lasts a few months or has been going on for years, you need to bridge the gap. You need a *new* identity. If only for the *meantime*. For example:

I am someone who is searching for my right livelihood.

I am an adventurer of life who has moved house and is seeking a just-right place to live.

A new identity gives you another safe anchor with which to firmly ground yourself in this unfamiliar territory. The key is choosing an identity that empowers you.

I am a person who was victimized by an evil boss who betrayed and humiliated me is not a choice that is likely to motivate and inspire you to move toward a new and more fulfilling trajectory. I say this tongue in cheek. I realize none of us would *consciously* choose this description. However, I have coached a number of clients who, after suffering a painful rejection or betrayal, have unwittingly taken on exactly this view of themselves.

There is another way—a way of reframing your situation into one that energizes you rather than keeps you feeling victimized. No matter how unfair or devastating your circumstances, dwelling in your story keeps you living there. The *unconscious* stories that we walk around telling ourselves through insidious mind chatter have a huge influence on our identities. This is why intentionally creating an inspiring new identity is so vital.

A new identity is tantamount to a spiritual intention. To allow a new door to open, it is vital to set an intention for where you are heading—for who you want to be. *Who* you want to be is your new destination. As Neale Donald Walsch puts it, you came here to create "the next grandest version of the greatest vision"[3] you ever had for who you are. You are the only one who can direct the unfolding of the most glorious vision of who you came here to be.

> *I am in transition—ready, willing, open, and able to create the*
> *next greatest vision of who I came here to be—feeling empowered!*

 ## Exercise: *Create Your New Identity*

Choose words that feel empowering. It is perfectly okay to write the facts of what you're going through. For example, *I am someone going through a divorce after thirty years of marriage.*

You may want to write a more expansive identity—one that reflects your relationship to your passions, your character or your view of life.

For example:

> *I am an exuberant lover of life. Or I am a fly fisherman. I am a bird lover.*
>
> *I am someone who loves to walk on the beach. I am pure love.*

Your sense of who you are will evolve and shift as you go through the exercises in this book. I invite you to stay open to expanding your view. Your soul and the Universal intelligence see you as pure magnificence! You are a multifaceted gem with many sparkling colors waiting to be expressed.

Feel free to write down one or as many identities as come to you.

> *I am …*

The Gift of the Dark Night

Sometimes our lives are so shaken up, we feel completely lost in the world of our current circumstances. We have no idea where we are headed. We may have an awe-inspiring spiritual awakening that transports us to the truth of who we really are. We realize that we have been asleep all this time. We look around and wonder where we fit.

It feels something like: *I am terrified, alone … searching for an answer. No solution feels right. I want to explore _x_, but maybe that's wrong. Others are saying I should do _y_, but that's not right for me either. Please, Universe, Spirit, God, anyone … help!*

This is where I found myself. I was still wedded to an inner belief that *every* marriage could be saved. Some part of me believed that there must be something that I, alone, could do to revive our bond, even if couple's counseling wasn't working. I began to realize that if I stayed attached to this belief, I could not free myself to follow my soul's path. My ego identity said divorce was *wrong* and that, "I am not a person who would get divorced. *I would never do that.*"

I knew that staying true to myself would mean disappointing not just my children but family and friends who appreciated spending time with us as an intact family. Our divorce would be an inevitable loss for them—a loss that all relatives and close friends suffer when a couple they love separates. Perhaps this is why some were not actively encouraging me to trust my heart. And my ego wanted nothing more than to make *everyone* happy.

At the same time, my soul was urging me to let go. This excruciating push-pull of my ego and soul led me into a "dark night of the soul."

In my experience, a dark night is actually the dissolving or death of an aspect of the ego. The ego, or conditioned self, is operating under a false belief. The ego believes that it is in charge of life's direction. It thinks that it can arrange everything in life—including other people's choices, comings and goings—in order to be loved, accepted, and approved of by the culture, peers, spouses, children, and community members.

The soul isn't actually having a dark night; the ego is! This *feels* like an unraveling, but in reality you are beginning to hear the true call of your soul. The soul is doing its work, patiently nudging, waking you up to a deeper truth about who you are. It is showing you, with a longing or a burning desire, what you've come here to experience or contribute to the world. In this vein, the soul is also revealing where you are out of integrity with your true self by shining a light on one or more areas of your life that aren't working.

The ego goes into a state of panic, despair, depression, or sorrow, because it cannot see a way out. It does not know how to reconcile the inner conflict of a deep desire paired with all the reasons it thinks it cannot have it. The only way through is to look at what is really true and right for you, in the *now*.

When I became aware that my soul had a different plan, I had to release my attachment to doing things the way our culture, and everyone I loved, for that matter, would want me to do them. As Gail confirmed, my marriage had died. I could not go about my life as I had been. No matter how much I distracted myself with the routines of daily life, I continued to feel the desire to spread my wings and fly. It was time to begin my next adventure.

I realized that my rule that I *should* be able to save my marriage was untenable. No one else was going to give me permission to dismantle this rule and other beliefs that were keeping me stuck and in great pain. Only I could hand over the key to the prison of my own creation. The truth is, as spiritual director Reverend Michael Bernard Beckwith says, "You are your own authority. The answer is inside of you."

I see now that it was actually a great blessing *not* to receive the permission from others that I was looking for. Had certain loved ones or my own cultural conditioning said, "We support you!" I would not have had to dig deeper to find the true authority within myself. Turning within was the process I needed to deepen my relationship with my own soul.

The more I asked and followed my own guidance, the stronger I became. I began to see myself with new eyes, as a spiritual being on a quest to live my most passionate purpose. As I expanded my view of who I was, I began to see myself as someone worthy of having new desires and meaningful contributions to make to the world. It was exciting! I realized that what I so desired, to share my deeply loving heart, was part of my gift to the world.

Another unexpected reward surfaced as well. Had I not taken the risk to let go of my marriage despite the family and cultural backlash, I would not have been as motivated to develop my coaching, speaking, and writing business. As the CEO of our family household, I had been working behind the scenes while my husband brought home the paycheck. In a purely practical way, the divorce confronted me with a need to financially support my daughters and myself. This got me out into the world in a bigger way—sharing my passion for spiritual growth and helping more people say yes to their dreams.

The truth is, no one else can give you permission to say yes to your deepest desires because no one else shares the intimate connection with your soul that you do. No one else can hear the quiet, middle-of-the-night whispers of your inner guidance or restless angst. Only a trusted partnership with the unconditionally loving and anchoring force of the soul can give you what you seek: the courage and trust to follow your true heart's path.

Letting the Soul Lead

In my dark night, the time finally came when I stopped trying to figure it out in the intellect.

I surrendered.

I decided to let my soul lead the way.

Rather than asking, what should I do or why is this happening, I began to wonder, *Who do I want to be*?

No matter what happens between us, I decided, I am going to be *loving*. Loving with everyone. My husband. People waiting in the grocery line. The postal clerk. In fact, I committed to myself, when I see a special quality in someone, I will share it with them. I began complimenting people whenever I noticed their inner or outer beauty. Their contagious smile, for example. This had a wonderful blooming effect on my spirit. With this practice of being loving, I began to feel my shyness melt away. I started experiencing a heart-opening love on a regular basis—even with people we call total strangers.

I also became acutely aware of when I was *not* being loving. This seemed to show up mostly in my relationships with my children, whom I adore and love more than anything in the world and would never want to harm in any way. When I lost my temper with my kids, as all parents do from time to time, I would feel tremendous guilt and sadness. As a result, I upped my practice. I consciously chose to cultivate the quality of being *loving* with my girls, no matter what emotions their actions or behavior triggered in me.

Once I made this pact, I had plenty of opportunities to practice!

I saw when I reacted out of frustration or fear rather than responding with tender care. Rather than berate myself for raising my voice, I began to shower myself with self-love and compassion. I knew this wasn't how I wanted to be, so why beat myself up when I fell down?!

Negative behaviors have their basis in the reactive patterns of the reptilian brain—the part of the brain that is subconsciously triggered into primal fight-or-flight behavior. To love the parts of you that you don't like is another alchemical tool. When you stop judging your actions, this alone creates a palpable shift.

My intention to be loving became the catalyst for phenomenal healing within me. The healing began with choosing how I wanted to act instead, and who I wanted to be with my children. What I knew for sure was that I wanted to *be love*.

The following exercise will help you bridge the gap between who you are now and who you desire to be.

Exercise: *Who Do You Choose to Be?*

Choosing who you want to be is like choosing your destiny's next stop. Where intention goes, energy will flow. By setting an intention to cultivate a soul quality, you are making a conscious choice to live in integrity and harmony with your soul.

Free, happy, empowered, courageous, at peace … these are all examples of soul qualities. You may have one or more qualities that you would like to activate in yourself. For the sake of ease and focus, I encourage you to begin with one.

Let your inner guidance give you the quality or emotion that will most move you forward.

I invite you now to pause and take a few deep breaths.

Breathe in peace on the inhale, and release everything else on the exhale.

Breathe in peace, and release the rest.

Do this for thirty seconds or until you feel calm and relaxed.

Now reflect on one quality or emotion that you would like to feel or experience more of in your life. What would empower you to make a decision or simply get unstuck? Put the words *I am* in front of your quality. For example, *I am happy*.

If you are having difficulty receiving guidance, become aware of what you *don't want* to be or feel. Take a moment to connect with your heart. What emotion are you feeling that you wish would go away? You may feel this emotion in your head or belly instead.

Tune into your body. Notice what you are feeling.

Name the emotion. For example, *I am feeling afraid*. Write it here:

I am …

Ask yourself, what do I want to feel instead? You may choose to feel the opposite of what you are feeling. For example, if you're feeling fear, you may want to feel brave instead. Other examples: *I am strong. I am powerful. I am relaxed. I am love. I am at peace.*

Your spirit knows the quality that your soul is ready to cultivate. Put one hand on your heart and ask, "What quality or emotion do I choose to feel *now*?" Your heart will tell you.

I am …

Post reminders of your intention in places where you will see them often—on the bathroom mirror, by your bedside, in your car. I love using sticky notes for this exercise. The more you see and repeat the words aloud, the more you will cultivate this quality of being in your everyday experience. When you find yourself acting in harmony with your intention, be sure to acknowledge and celebrate your wins!

This is you, turning to GOLD.

3

 Your Heart Knows

Don't ask what the world needs. Ask what makes you come alive, and go do it. Because what the world needs is people who have come alive.

~ Howard Thurman

It is encoded in your soul to create heaven on earth. You can give more attention to the spark in your heart—to your inspiration—and to loving yourself and others, because you are love. Your soul knows this truth. Inspired action is your road to heaven now.

~ A Journal Entry

Desire ignites your heart and launches your ideas and dreams into life so they can take form. Even a tiny spark of desire can get you unstuck and moving again. In fact, desire is so powerful that it can wake you up to a whole new perception of who you are and what you are capable of creating.

Everything you have ever manifested in your life began as a seed of desire. Desire may arrive as a yearning or longing, or a deep knowing that you are here to express and contribute something more—something of meaning to the world. Becoming aware of your heart's desire is key to your happiness because your passion is the force of all creation. Over and over, I have seen my own inspired desires shake up my life just enough to come fully alive again.

I first experienced the power of desire in a life-changing way just weeks before my college graduation from UC Santa Barbara. I had been thoroughly engaged in my political science studies and was proud of my academic success. Still, I could not imagine myself looking for a "real job" or attending graduate school right away because nothing in those realms appealed to me. I very much wanted a fulfilling career, but I had no clear direction.

Adventure was calling my heart. An adventure like my close college friend Jeanne had taken years earlier. Jeanne had made a bold move. She'd taken a year's leave from school and moved to Jackson Hole, Wyoming, to ski and wait tables. I remember being in awe when she drove out to a ski resort where she knew no one, landed a job, and fulfilled her dream, knowing that her parents would probably not approve of her mid-college leave. With her contagious zest for life, she had written to me often about her new friends and how much fun she was having.

Following in Jeanne's footsteps, I envisioned myself gliding down ski slopes by day and making good tips at night to pay the rent in the stunning Colorado Rockies. I'd spent one summer in Vail as a nanny when I was thirteen, so I had fond memories of the beautiful resort village. Still, making a solo move all these years later was intimidating. I would need to find a well-paying job to cover the high cost of famous ski-town living. I had no contacts to help connect me with a job or housing. What was I thinking? To most people it seemed a little crazy! But Jeanne's courage propelled me forward. If she could do it, maybe I could too!

My fear kept talking. What if I couldn't find a job? What if I didn't make any new friends? What if I drove the four-day road trip there alone (this part truly terrified me), didn't succeed, and had to turn around and come back to my mom's house with nothing to show for it? All of these possibilities flashed through my mind. But the exciting possibility of succeeding was more compelling. Having always been the good, responsible student, I needed to break out of my mold and do something that, for me, felt both scary and exhilarating.

As graduation approached, I was literally down to a few dollars, and I still had no idea how this adventure was going to come together. I still needed a job, a place to live, money to live on until I found work, and a car to get there!

I continued to hold the vision of my ski adventure. I saw and felt myself moving gracefully through the pine trees, gliding down sunny slopes through soft, powdery snow. Then, literally one week before graduation, I received a serendipitous phone call. A women's charitable foundation I'd never heard of, the Santa Barbara City Club, formed to fight for women's right to vote, was on the line. "We are gifting you with a $4000 merit scholarship," my angel of the moment announced. I fell into a happy state of shock. This was truly a magical surprise that I could not have possibly predicted. I hadn't even applied for their award—or anyone else's. Not only that, but it was free money to use however I wanted—with no strings attached. Who gives no-strings-attached money to a graduating college student to do whatever her heart desires—including deep powder skiing?!

The Universe, of course.

In an instant and truly out of the blue, my 1970 Volkswagen Bug and first month's living expenses were funded!

Looking back, the key to manifesting this dream was *trusting* my desire. I didn't focus on or stress about how I was going to get the resources to make it happen. My desire was strong enough that I just kept affirming that somehow, some way, *I am moving to Vail.*

It never occurred to me that I was not making the move. I had a clear vision, and a clear direction fueled by desire is a potent force. Studies from the Institute of HeartMath show that the heart, our seat of desire, is 5000 times more powerful than the brain.[4] From our passion and enthusiasm, the heart generates a magnetic energy field that helps us manifest our inspired vision.[5] The Universe cannot help but respond to this kind of power with all kinds of assistance.

As I kept my focus on what I wanted, my continued affirmation of this desire turned into a feeling that I've come to experience as a *just know*. I got the same feeling when I felt inspired to apply to law school. I also just knew when I had my stand-up comedy dream that I had to follow through and try it. Something in me was ignited by the challenge and possibility of succeeding. It *felt* right. All of these desires came from a deeper call—a call from my soul.

In my experience, these *just know* feelings are the soul's way of guiding us toward our destinies. They often begin as a tiny spark: *Wouldn't it be fun to … !*

Another guiding clue is feeling inspired when a friend or colleague takes a risk to live *their* passion. We might even feel a mix of joy and envy, wishing we had the resources—or guts—to pull off such an adventure, career change, or out-of-the-box endeavor.

If I had not paid attention to my inspiration and stayed open to my ski dream, I would have let the opportunity pass. I remember wondering if I "should" be seeking a professional job instead. But nothing "respectable" in the conventional sense even remotely appealed to me, and I have since learned to trust the feeling of being called by enthusiasm. What enthuses you, what lights you up, is your soul speaking loud and clear. The word enthusiasm comes from the Greek word *entheos*, which means the God within. Truly the soul acts as a God within when enthusiasm shows up to usher you forward on your path.

It turns out that my move to Vail was not just about powder skiing in the Rockies. My linear mind's goal was to bridge the gap between college graduation and graduate school. But the Universe had much more in mind than I could imagine. Within four months of landing in Vail, I met and fell in love with my future husband. We joined to bring into being our two beautiful daughters. My soul obviously knew what it was doing. It sent me to Colorado to meet, in time, the two greatest loves of my life.

Over and over, I have experienced this phenomenon. Saying yes to a true heart's desire always seems to reveal a hidden treasure that surfaces in the process of going for it. Invariably, unexpected gifts have shown up that were not part of the outcome I was envisioning.

Your soul is the supreme architect, pouring over the grand plans of your dream life. It sits high upon a sunny hilltop with a 360-degree view of your majestic possibilities. Meanwhile, all you are sometimes privy to is a barely lit entryway with a little sign overhead that reads:

Just Say Yes!

Romancing Your Inner Muse

Your relationship with your soul is like the beginning of a sweet and passionate romance. Romance begins with being open. Romance asks you to be open to seeing life and your circumstances, even your pain, with new eyes.

Your bond with your soul is the most sacred, intimate bond you will ever cultivate. Your soul accepts you fully just as you are, including your so-called flaws and weaknesses. Your soul blesses the details that you may judge about your life, including the messiness of things that you wish you could change but cannot. Your soul's love for you is truly unconditional. This love is so expansive and pure that it is sometimes beyond our human comprehension to perceive its sheer magnitude. We each have the natural ability to cultivate and feel the sheer bliss and devotion our soul has for us.

I feel my soul's love for me most palpably during times of meditation and conscious dialoguing in my journal. You may feel it when you are out in nature or looking into your lover's eyes. Feeling emotionally moved is a sign that you are connecting with this deeper part of yourself. Joy, passion, ecstasy, happiness, and peace are all emotions that stream from love. Any time you are in a geographic location that resonates deeply with your soul, you will feel this sweet connection with your inner loving guide as well.

For example, in this moment I am writing in an open-air, artsy, apricot-and-sapphire painted café in Puerto Vallarta, one block from the ocean. I am sipping a Mexican-bean espresso topped with frothy foamed milk. I am thrilled to have found this comforting writer's haven. Being here is feeding my passion for the new and exotic. My spirit is *singing* inside.

From the minute I stepped out of the airport and took in the tropical, sweet-and-spicy-scented warm air, my body relaxed and my heart opened. I love this place! I am staying in the romantic zone of Viejo Vallarta (meaning Old Town) in a complex of gorgeous white stucco buildings with terra cotta tile roofs. Flower-lined pathways are filled with brilliant yellow and salmon-pink flowers, and delicate bougainvillea in multicolored clusters of light pink, white, fuchsia, purple, and red fill the window boxes. Since I grew up in southern California with bougainvillea at the entrance to our home and I now live in Seattle where it's too cold to grow, seeing these vines all over the complex here brings me instantly home.

Add to all this colorful beauty and luscious scents, romantic strolling musicians, golden glowing sunsets every evening, and walks on the beach at dusk. All of my senses are receiving beauty on every level of sight, sound, scent, and touch.

As I take in this beauty through every aspect of my being, it feels as though every cell of my body is celebrating! My spirit wants to run down the beach exclaiming, "I am so happy!" This joyous moment of celebration is my soul's way of telling me: *this* is what I desire.

My bliss and your bliss may look as different as chamomile tea and a quadruple shot of high-octane espresso on ice. What might make me want to strut naked through my favorite coffee shop singing, "Hallelujah, hallelujah, hallelujah, I'm free, free, free at last!" is very possibly something completely different from your happy-dance motivator. (I am partly kidding. I really don't have the desire to strut naked through any public place, although the prospect of dancing and singing, "Hallelujah, I'm free!" does make my heart swell with joy.) But you get my point. Our individual passions are as varied as our unique soul paths. It's not about *what* you love, it's about *knowing* what you love.

 Exercise: *Claim Your Bliss*

Now you:

What do you love? What brings you alive?

 Relax and take a few deep breaths.

 Let go of everything that came before this moment.

 Come into the present.

 Put one hand on your heart and connect with your loving spirit.

The following questions will help you get in touch with your heart's desire:

- What makes your heart sing?

- When do you feel most connected to your heart or soul?

- What places ignite your passion?

- Who in your life inspires you? This might be a friend, mentor, teacher, author, mythic figure—living or not.

- What turns you on about who they are or what they do?

If I Couldn't Possibly Fail, I Would …

Often clients initially come to me saying something like, "I don't know what I'm passionate about. I seem to have lost my zest for life." If your passion feels buried under emotions of regret, anger, sadness, or loss, know that your enthusiasm for life is simply being camouflaged. Underneath these emotions is a spark of desire waiting to be ignited and expressed.

Your soul is always speaking to you, giving you nudges of desire. Your ego, on the other hand, is adept at throwing cold water on any desire that would bring you true joy and happiness. This is because the ego's job is to preserve the status quo. The ego falsely believes it must figure out how to bring your desires into manifestation, yet it is not capable of doing so. The ego balks because it fears it can't make what you desire real. And it is right.

Only the heart has the powerful magnetic field, as well as the creative capacity, to attract the resources, people, and things needed to realize your desires. Your heart is the voice of your guiding genius. Keeping the focus on your heart is your paramount responsibility. However, since you are human, you do go in and out of being side-tracked by your ego.

Sometimes the ego is so loud that it drowns out the voice of the soul. In truth, your passions are being registered in your awareness, even if you are not conscious of it. What I notice is that my clients usually *do* know what their hearts want. They have just often ruled out the possibility of having what they want before the seed of desire has had a chance to take root. The ego, citing lack of money, lack of time, lack of energy, or too many responsibilities, has blindly mowed over their dreams like a bulldozer wiping out a meadow of soon-to-bloom wildflowers.

When the ego is doing its best to distract you from your heart, engaging your mindful awareness is a great tool. Being mindful is like inviting a solid, loyal friend who sees your sparkling potential to survey the situation with loving, neutral eyes. Like having a comforting fairy godmother listen to all the noes going on inside your head, chuckle wisely, and point out that they're just not true. You have this loving observer inside of you. You can activate the inner wise witness with intention.

Here's how it works: Begin to simply observe what your ego is saying in response to your desire. In other words, another way to become aware of your soul's messages is to listen to your ego's excuses.

A good one to start with is perfectionism. Notice what you keep putting off because you're afraid that it—or you—won't be good enough. The scared ego withholds satisfaction and praise on the basis that *everything can always be improved.* Listen for words like, "Good try … but it's not quite right …" Or, "I'd really love to _____, but I'd have to study for years to be competent at it."

Blame is another juicy one. The ego likes to blame others for its lack of follow-through: "If my spouse, boss, child (you fill in the blank) was not in my way, I would _____." In every excuse lies a golden possibility—an opportunity for more alchemy as you turn your dross into gold.

What would you say yes to if time, money, responsibilities, or insufficient resources were not at issue?

The ego says this is a silly question—that the limitations are real—that this is simply *reality* talking. If this is what you're hearing, note what this so-called voice of reality is telling you. Be the witness of your own inner dialogue. As you do, you will begin to become aware of how you respond to your heart's impulses, and what you really *do* want. Allow yourself to be open. Write in your journal the possibilities that delight you even if they seem like impossible pipe dreams.

In my experience, the biggest mistake we make is stamping out the sparks of enthusiasm and desire before they have a chance to catch fire. We forget that we are not responsible for figuring out how our desires will manifest in reality. Our domain is to focus on and nurture our desires into being.

This takes a bit of faith. It takes a willingness to play with possibilities before you have any evidence of them becoming real. By imagining, visualizing, and feeling the emotions of your desire happening, you light the fire in your belly. You begin to feel the spark of something more, something better, emerging. Positive emotions ignite stronger desire and a fuller enthusiasm. Soon your enthusiasm catalyzes a wave of momentum and catches fire in the heart. An ignited heart is truly a force to reckon with. The Universe cannot help but respond with favorable assistance. This is what Canadian author and pastor Basil King was referring to when he said, "Be bold and mighty forces will come to your aid." [6]

 ### Exercise: *A Life of No Regrets*

Our desires flow from our values—what matters most to us. I invite you to pause here.

Relax and take a few deep breaths.

Breathe in and out for thirty seconds.

Let your body fully relax.

Drop your shoulders.

Soften the muscles in your face.

Relax your belly.

Feel the support of the floor beneath your feet.

Sense and feel yourself fully supported by your own higher self, God, or the Universe.

Take a moment to imagine me there with you, cheering you on with love and encouragement.

Now imagine that you have lived out your years here on earth. Your life is coming to a peaceful conclusion. Perhaps you pass in your sleep, with loved ones all around you, giving you the nurturing and support you need to transition.

Even if you don't believe in life after death or that the soul goes on after you pass, allow yourself to pretend for a moment for the purpose of this exercise. Assume that when we leave our bodies we journey to "the other side," where we examine the dreams, desires and intentions we had for our life and ourselves. Imagine now that you are now sitting in front of a supportive "life review committee." They ask you just one question:

Looking back on your life, is there anything that you wish you had done?

Take a few moments to reflect on this question. If you were to create a life of few or no regrets, what would it include? Do not get stuck on *how* to make it happen. For now, let yourself simply become aware of your desires.

If regrets surface, you may want to write them down as well. Witness them like a loving fairy godmother or trusted wise guide, but don't let them sidetrack you from connecting with what you desire now.

Imagine now that you are looking back on your days. Connect to your heart and inner wisdom. Let it guide you in answering the following:

- To feel fulfilled and satisfied, I would need to …

- When my life is complete, something I would like to hear others say about me is …

- If I couldn't possibly fail I would …

It's Never Too Late to Follow Your Heart

When you need to have a certain result come from your desire, this is a sign that the desire is motivated by an ego goal rather than by your soul. Ego goals come from your conditioned self's ambition—the part of you that believes you have to work hard, struggle, and strive to get the results you want. The very nature of an ego goal is the need to get somewhere or achieve something.

A soul-inspired desire, by contrast, has its own intrinsic reward. With a true heart's desire, you feel drawn to pursue the activity, project, or relationship regardless of the outcome. You might still want a specific result, but you would do it for the joy, meaning, or fulfillment even if that outcome did not materialize.

There is nothing wrong with ego goals, but they tend to require hard work to bring to fruition because they do not originate in the heart. They either come from a sense of scarcity, fear, doubt, or worry, or from the desire to have something so that you can feel better about your life. Because these kinds of desires do not flow from your soul's inspiration, they also do not allow you to be carried by powerful Universal assistance.

Not only that, but ambitions without heart often leave you feeling deflated and exhausted after all that striving. Living from ambition takes its toll over time. At a certain point, you may look back on your life and see that you've been going from one ego goal to another, striving to achieve.

I once coached a lawyer, Christy, who came to me seeking clarity on whether her law practice could give her the fulfillment her soul was longing for. Christy's story is similar to that of many bright, well-meaning lawyers I've coached—sincere and lovely people with big, caring hearts—who attended law school for the financial security it promised and now feel empty, apathetic, stuck, or adrift.

I asked Christy what she liked about her practice with a large law firm. It took her a while to respond. Upon reflection, she found that she worked very hard for a relatively few fleeting moments of celebration with her colleagues when they would win a case. Day-to-day, her work was punctuated more by stress than meaningful satisfaction. She often found that wrapping up a case brought more of a sense of *relief* than true fulfillment.

She also got in touch with what did bring her joy. Spending more time with her children and having a flexible schedule that would allow her to work from her home were high on her list. Christy felt grief about having missed significant moments of her daughter's early years, and she did not want to have the same regret with her young son. Her soul also desired more creative expression, meaning, and passion. It was clear to me that her inner wisdom was guiding her away from ambition-based ego goals. Working to be productive and earn a paycheck was not enough to feed her growth.

Christy did not have to leave the law to sustain her heart. She continues to work as an attorney, but on her own schedule and from home. She set up a solo practice and only takes cases that bring her true satisfaction.

Christy's biggest fear, that her firm would feel betrayed when she left, did not come to pass. Once she became clear that she needed to move on, nearly all of her colleagues were supportive. "How did you do it?" One even privately knocked on her office door to find out her secret for saying yes.

 Exercise: *From Fear to Fulfillment*

This exercise is an adaptation of a powerful process I learned from spiritual teacher Sonia Choquette. When guiding clients through this exercise, they express their truth out loud. You can do it this way or in writing.

- Take a moment to consult your heart. Is there a decision or situation you are contemplating that brings up fear?

- Focusing on this circumstance, go ahead and list your fears. Getting them out of your head and onto the page is cathartic and healing. What stays in our head keeps repeating. When you voice it or write it down and let it go, a lightening occurs. With the following prompt, dump your fears until you feel a release.

Regarding this decision or situation …

I'm afraid of …

I'm afraid of …

I'm afraid of …

- Now take a deep breath and imagine that the fears have melted off your body and fallen into the earth.

- Put one hand on your heart and answer, in the same way as above …

  My true voice says …

  My true voice says …

  My true voice says …

The Desire Underneath All Desire

When I began searching for my passion, I was determined to find meaningful work that I loved. I spent hours devouring self-growth books. I'd find a book and a cozy spot on the floor in the self-help aisle and be completely happy losing myself in this new land of how-to-discover-my-bliss. I knew what I wanted to feel; I just didn't know how to get there. I knew that I wanted my work to not feel like work at all. I wanted it to feel like play.

A whole new side of me came alive when I began teaching spiritual growth workshops and coaching clients. My inner creative child was cheering, and my heart felt calm and at peace. I began to feel the immense joy of living my passion. I loved connecting with people on issues of the heart and soul—on what really mattered to them—because this was the stuff on which their happiness depended.

I loved being fully present, listening deeply, and helping people connect with their own emotions, while guiding them to clarity. I felt many moments of sheer bliss. Over and over, I experienced rewarding exchanges of deep connection with my clients and class participants. One day, I paused, took in a deep breath, and exhaled. I noticed that *I was doing it*. I had found work I loved. I was living my dream! Waves of ecstatic joy rippled through me and brought me to tears.

At the same time, though, I noticed that certain aspects of my work caused me stress and angst. For example, I would conceive of a workshop, make up a flyer announcing it, and before I could begin distributing the announcement, worry would set in.

"What if nobody comes?" "What if I invest in a rental space and don't get enough registrants to cover my expenses?" In the background, I heard the inner critic wailing away, "Enough to cover your expenses—you need more than that! You've got to make a living! What if you can't be financially successful doing this?!"

Knowing that our thoughts powerfully affect the reality that manifests, I would then fear that I was sabotaging my own success with doubts and worry. To add insult to injury, as they say, I was afraid of being afraid! My fear that the outcome would not be what I desired zapped the joy I wanted to feel. It was a huge energy drain. Here I was genuinely living my passion for spiritual growth, but my own pattern of worry and fear was taking the fun out of marketing my classes.

Noticing this stress on a regular basis brought me to another turning point. I realized that I was making myself miserable with thoughts of fear and doubt. I saw how I was allowing my happiness to be dependent on external events that I could not control. If a workshop sold out, I felt happy and victorious. However, if only a few people signed up, I allowed myself to feel discouraged and sometimes distressed about my future ability to create successful events.

One day, I heard Wayne Dyer speak about the power of intention. He said that we needed only one intention to radically transform our lives for the better: the intention to feel good. I got the *yes* feeling that told me this was a powerful truth. I made another clear decision.

> *I decided that no matter what was happening in my world, my
> first priority was to feel good.*

If something was upsetting me, this was a reminder to return to my intention and ask myself, what do I need to feel good right now?

When I finally put my well-being first, before having anything, my life began to change. I lightened up. I realized, with real eyes, that pinning my happiness on some future event was robbing me of the joy I could be having now. Each time I had expectations about how an endeavor should turn out, I was, in effect, living in the future, when being in the present is the only way to experience true happiness.

Before this point, when I didn't get the results I wanted, I would worry that I was doing something "wrong." I thought I needed to fix my situation or myself.

The truth, however, is that none of us needs fixing. Nor could we be fixed if we tried! This is only the ego's misguided perspective. From the soul's point of view, we are healthy, whole, and complete. If something feels off or wrong, it means we are looking at it through the eyes of the ego, rather than through the eyes of the soul. The soul knows that we are perfect just as we are.

The good news is, positive change in our circumstances comes not from shifting our situation but from altering our perception of it.

So I changed my perception. I returned to my heart and connected to my original desire for my work: to uplift and empower people to be free to follow their hearts.

I decided to stay focused on my passion, my true reason for doing this work, regardless of how many people show up. Yes, I needed to earn a living. However, judging myself as unsuccessful when my income did not match my expectations was not working to bring in the income I desired anyway! My own self-judgments actually made me feel inadequate and deficient, hardly a recipe for attracting financial abundance.

My new plan was to enjoy the process of my work from start to finish. I vowed to come to my classes and marketing with joy for the work itself, and let the Universe handle the rest. As long as I showed up fully engaged in my purpose and passion, the outcome was none of my business.

I could—and did—visualize the results I desired. I imagined my workshops being lively and full, with everyone attending, including me, feeling connected and in flow. Then I let go. How many showed up would be what it would be. To feel free and happy, I had to release what I could not control. Not surprisingly, I stopped taking my "success" and myself so seriously—and began to have a lot more fun.

Feeling Happy No Matter What

In my experience, the decision to be happy, no matter what goes down (or up) in life, is not a shift that comes easily. How good we feel tends to vary depending on what is happening in our outer world—our external reality. At least this is how we've been conditioned to see and experience life.

You may find it challenging to wrap your mind around this notion of feeling happy no matter what. You may have a hard time even imagining that you could relax and let go—even when life is handing you "stuff" you didn't order and wish you could send back to the universal storehouse of things, situations, and people you don't need or want. For example, have you ever wished you could just say f**k it, and let yourself enjoy the day anyway? [7]

Everything shifts when you wake up to the truth that your well-being is the basic foundation of all that you create in life. All the "real-world" essentials, including the basics of home, food, and loving relationships, come out of this foundation of feeling good. To think you can have a wonderful life without putting your inner happiness and peace first is an illusion.

We usually have to experience a certain amount of pain before we realize that *we* are more important than anything that does or does not transpire in our lives. However, if we continue to allow our well-being to be determined by our reactions

to other people, situations, and events, it is like living on a constantly running emotional roller coaster. When things are going our way, we are happy. When something
doesn't go according to plan or someone disappoints us, we let it take us down. This
is not a recipe for a good life because, as the old Yiddish saying goes, "We plan and
God laughs." No matter how much we try to dictate the order of our days, life has its
own divine order and it often does not consult us first before changing the menu—or
the bill!

I'm sure you've heard the phrase, happiness is an inside job. True and lasting
contentment can only be sourced from within. Our life experiences reflect our *inner*
landscapes. Life doesn't happen randomly *to* us. Life is more like a movie script that
we are playing out. And whether we are conscious of it or not, we are the scriptwriters!

Perhaps because I stepped into the next chapter of my life as a single person, I
have been in a perfect position to see that I am the sole creator of my life experience.
I've had no life partner to blame when things aren't going my way. Since I also
became an entrepreneur at the same time, I have no boss to point the finger at either.
And recently my youngest left the nest to attend college. Now I can't hold my kids
responsible either.

I do not mean to say that we should deny our genuine emotions. Far from it.
As I wrote earlier, feeling our emotions is absolutely vital to the process of digesting
the disappointments that inevitably surface. As human beings, we will experience
sadness, anger, sorrow, grief, and more, as well as the uplifting emotions of joy, happiness, peace, and ecstasy. This is all part of the juicy adventure of being alive.

Committing to being happy no matter what is a radically life-changing choice.
Actually, I should call it a practice, because practice it requires. Not just daily, but
moment to moment. It is a decision to raise your consciousness to the next level—to
become conscious of a spiritual law—that everything in your external life is temporary and impermanent. Even relationships that last an entire lifetime go through ups
and downs and must grow and change to endure.

Few of us have just one career or one love relationship, or feel successful in everything we undertake. Still, the limited ego believes that these structures should last
forever, that other people should respond to us in certain ways, and that as long as
we are "good" people and do the "right" things, life should give us what we want. The
truth is, the one thing we cannot control is the impermanent nature of life itself.

Our work, our relationships, our destinies have a timing of their own that we are not necessarily privy to. We can, however, control how we digest changes and endings. And here's where our power as spiritual beings lies. We get to choose. We can choose to see life through a new, more joy-affirming lens. The lens of: *Life wants me to be happy. Life loves me, even when it appears that things are not going well. Whatever is before me is just a temporary phase. This too shall pass.*

Commitments made from a sincere intention to create happiness from within are the most powerful of decisions. What could be more authentic and fulfilling than the decision to feel good regardless of what is happening in the outer world?

To feel happy no matter what is the ultimate freeing decision.

4

 Happiness Is Here

Remember to delight yourself first, then others can be truly delighted.

~ SARK

How much are you willing to fall in love with you? Nothing is more important than your well-being—than feeling good.

~ A Journal Entry

Finding work I loved was one part of my vision for my new life. The other part was attracting a partner to share my life. If I am really honest with myself, I have to say that I *longed* to have a mutually-loving, reciprocal relationship with a soul mate. This yearning was so deep that I could not imagine my life without being partnered.

After moving to my own home, I dated a number of interesting people and learned a lot from each relationship, but none of these was "the one." When I consulted from time to time with my trusted Jungian counselor, John Joseph, the subject would often come up. "Do you see me attracting a life partner any time soon?" I would ask John. Then one session he responded in his compassionate yet straightforward way, "I have to be honest with you, Betsy. Underneath your desire for a romantic partner is the sense of *I'll be happy when* _____."

"I'm sorry," I said. "Can you explain what you mean?" I didn't understand what he was getting at.

"It's as though you feel that you need something outside of you, like a partner, to be truly happy," he went on. "Ohhhh," I replied. "Well that's because I *do*! I want a loving partner to share my life with more than anything else."

And then he said, "It *appears* that what is keeping you from fulfillment is a missing partner. But this is an illusion. It's not true. You can find the same love you're longing for—within yourself. In other words, what you desire is deep, loving communion with your own soul. We can experience this same feeling with a lover or spouse, but we do not *need* another person to have this. As soon as you feel complete within yourself, you will be available to attract the kind of soul-connected partnership you desire. A loving companion will be the icing on the cake for you."

These were not the words I wanted to hear.

At the time, John's counsel made me feel frustrated. Intellectually, I understood what he meant. Even the most vibrant, loving partnership cannot bring us true satisfaction unless we first feel fulfilled within ourselves. Many times I'd heard people say, "When you fully love yourself, the right person for you will show up." Honestly, I had tired of hearing it. I believed that I loved myself as much as I possibly could. "How much more love can I give to me?" I thought. I want to share my heart with another person! I had a longing to experience deep, intimate sharing with a partner— the feeling of total oneness with another—something I had primarily experienced while in the throes of romantic love.

Yes, I did have ecstatic moments of communion with my soul in meditation. I had felt this connected bliss on numerous occasions. But I wanted real-life, real-time companionship with a real person. If we are spiritual beings having a human experience, affection and touch are two key joys of being in a human body! Communing, relating, and sharing moments of connection with a partner are some of life's most satisfying gifts. I had delightful visions of my partner and I laughing, cooking and eating delicious food, dancing, creating art, exchanging ideas, making love, and having many exciting adventures traveling the world together.

Despite my argument, I see now that John was right in one very important respect. I was not just *desiring* a life partner. I was longing—and *waiting*—for one to show up. It was as though some part of me was on hold. I was living for a future event to occur in order to be truly content.

I am not alone in projecting my happiness out to some future event like a better job, place to live, or more spiritually evolved spouse. It is very human of us to want more. The problem is when we *wait* for more. I call it a trick of the ego. We find ourselves either focused in the past, pining away for something we once had but lost, or living in the future, pinning our happiness on some elusive possibility that we are convinced will bring us perfect bliss. Living in the past or the future, we miss out on life in the present. *Which means we're missing out on life altogether, because we can only be in this moment.*

John gently pointed out this red flag in my own thinking. I had been married for so many years that I could not imagine my life *without* a partner. I had fallen into a rut of believing I could only experience this deep soul connection in one form, which made it challenging to even envision feeling fulfilled in other ways. My ego was attached to my life looking a certain way: me living with my loving partner in a traditional relationship. I was trapping myself in this picture of "how things should be."

The best part of desires not showing up is the gift the delay inevitably brings. After five years of wanting and seeking what continued to elude me, I finally let go. I was forced to either surrender or be miserable. Since I prefer happiness and freedom to misery any day, I chose the former. The process of seeking was no longer making me happy. I was tired of looking outside of myself—and tired of waiting—for a man to come along and enrich my life.

I had come to another important turning point. I knew what I wanted, but it wasn't here! It was obvious to me that focusing on what was missing wasn't making me feel good, so why would I continue staring at this void in my life?

I was finally ready to take charge of creating my own happiness, with or without a partner. I had chosen to be happy no matter what, and this had to include my love life as well.

Loving Right Where You Are

Once I made the decision to stop waiting for my partner to appear, I began to look within. I did a lot of searching through my belief system. I had weeded out the belief that *I can't have what I want*. Something subtler was lurking beneath the surface. I asked myself, What am I seeing as wrong with my current situation? What emotion is being single causing me to feel? It came bubbling up to the surface like nasty crude oil threatening to desecrate the pristine Alaskan waters. Shame. I felt shame for still living solo. My inner critical voice said, "It's been five years, and I should be partnered by now."

I thought about this. Knowing our truth sets us free. It is more than worthwhile to question our own thinking, beliefs, and assumptions. Finding out if what we've been telling ourselves is really true is a freedom-giving exercise.

We have to allow our inner advocate, our truth-seeking detective, to step in and investigate. Donning the cloak of this wise observer self, I asked, "Is it really true that there is something wrong with being single?"

The answer, of course, was absolutely not! It was only my own judgment on my status that was causing me pain. Others may believe this, but whatever judgments they might have about my single identity, I certainly did not have to take them on.

Not only that, but, as I discuss in Chapter Two, we are each free to create our own identity. And to set ourselves free to follow our destiny, we are *charged* with doing so. Beyond our identities and roles is the beautiful truth of who we really are—the essence of who we're being and who we want to be.

What's more, we cannot create or manifest anything that is not within the scope of our assumed identity to do, be, or have. In other words, if I am unable to see myself as happy while living solo, I have no chance to be. I have completely closed out the possibility of happiness right where I am.

Sometimes the roles we have assigned ourselves or taken on from the culture just don't work for us anymore. The role of being single was that way for me. Why was I even identifying with this culturally-established category of married versus single? I had to wonder. Clearly it wasn't bringing me joy to do so. The truth about who I am is so much broader. In my essence, I am love.

Gift number one of my partner not yet materializing: seeing myself with new eyes. I was given the opportunity to enlarge my vision of who I am to include even greater expressions of love.

I am not single, I decided. I am love.

I am capable of feeling, giving, and receiving love for others and myself in every moment. Not surprisingly, I see this as essential to my purpose. I am capable of generating loving exchanges—even with people I don't know—in the grocery line, at the credit union, and even on the phone with my cell phone carrier's customer service person. I felt love calling me to do so. If love is what my heart so longs to express, share, and contribute to a partner, I can be love *now*. I don't have to wait until "the one" knocks on my door to share my heart.

And waiting, as I spoke about earlier, doesn't work anyway. Being what we desire is the way to touch what our heart wants. We attract what we want by embodying its *essence* now—in the present.

The greatest freedom is accepting and loving ourselves, just as we are. To love our quirks and idiosyncrasies and everything we might find wrong with who and where we are in our lives, this is the ultimate act of self-love. It's not easy, but I believe it is the crux of the journey to become real.

 Exercise: *Loving Yourself Right Where You Are*

I love that we can be the detectives of our own psyches. That we can look around our vast and glorious inner landscapes to see where we might be judging ourselves as wrong or inadequate.

The healing can begin by simply checking in and asking: Where am I not being loving or kind to me?

I invite you to rate your happiness on a scale of 0 to 10, with 0 being very unhappy and 10 being ecstatically happy. Your body knows your truth. Tune in to your gut and your heart and let your body give you a number.

On a scale of 0 to 10, I rate my happiness as _____.

When you tune in to how happy or unhappy you feel, what situation comes to mind? Usually you are evaluating your happiness based on something that is or is not happening in your life. Truly, sometimes it does feel like nothing is going well. But often there is one particular area of life where we would most like to see a positive change. *Where in your life would you most like to experience a shift?*

For example, for me, it was my love life.

- What is it for you?

- Now, focusing on this situation, this area of life you wish were different, ask yourself: Where am I not being loving or kind to myself?

- What might you be holding against yourself?

- In what ways are you withholding love and acceptance from yourself?

If you're not sure, spend a few minutes journaling.

Now look over your answers. Whatever comes up, remember that it is not who you are. *It is just a story.* For example, deep down I was telling myself that being single meant there was something wrong with me. This story was causing me to harbor shame against myself. And it wasn't true. By continuing to tell myself this, even unconsciously, I was being unkind to myself.

When you shine light on your own version of your story, on how you are condemning yourself, you can see the un-truth in it and let it go. Holding on to stories that make you feel small, inadequate, or unloved has the effect of beating yourself up daily. Are you ready to free yourself from self-inflicted pain?

Look back over your answers to the questions above. Connect with your wise heart, your soul, and ask: Is this *really* true?

The last step is forgiving yourself for believing in your story or un-truth.

For example, in my case, I voiced, "I forgive myself for believing that there is something wrong with me because I am still single."

Now you:

Complete the following question. You may have one or several stories bubble up. Like the example above, write a forgiveness statement for each story.

- I forgive myself for believing …

- I forgive myself for believing …

- I forgive myself for believing …

Seeing Your Past With New Eyes

One day, I called into the talk radio show of one of my favorite spiritual-growth authors, Dr. Christiane Northrup. "I've been divorced for five years, and I am so ready for my transition to be over," I shared. What I meant was, I thought my new, wonderful husband would be here by now and I would be resuming partnered life.

With her signature candor and grace, Dr. Northrup jumped in with the story of her own divorce transition: "A good friend pulled me aside one day and told me it was time to stop telling my divorce story. My friend suggested I write a love letter to my husband, thanking him for the gifts of our relationship—*and then let the past go*."

As you can probably guess, Dr. Northrup gave me her prescription. "It's time to write a love letter to your past. Not to send or read to your ex-husband, unless you believe he will receive it with love. You'll know if it feels right. If not, read it to a friend who will honor your sharing as the heartfelt gift that it is. You need a witness. To have our stories witnessed is very important for healing and releasing the past."

I knew her advice was spot on. I poured my heart into my assignment. I ended up with a seven-page letter, detailing the highlights of our courtship and twenty-two years together, including our very first romantic dinner and the births of our precious daughters. I then read the letter to a dear friend, who was visibly touched and gave me the exquisite gift of her witnessing.

Writing this letter to my former husband was as good as writing it to myself. New feelings of appreciation for this chapter of our life together welled up in me. I experienced the innocence and truth of our love again, without leveling judgment onto a past that didn't continue into the future. I felt so happy! It felt wonderful to revive all those loving feelings again. I felt tremendous gratitude for each and every positive experience chronicled in my letter.

I knew our daughters were the primary gift of our relationship, but this exercise showed me something more as well. We had been through a number of "firsts" to-gether. I met him when I was just twenty-two. We had been through a lot together. After a couple of years of trying to save our marriage, I had initiated the divorce, and he had been angry for some time. I had allowed his anger to negatively affect me and my view of our time together, but the letter shifted this. It felt much better to step back and see the bigger picture of our relationship—to see the true gifts that this life chapter had given us and our children. Honoring the past allowed me to reclaim the treasure of our two decades together once again.

I felt a huge breath of air waft in and refresh the chamber of my heart. It felt as if my life was being renewed. Energetically, I closed the door with a clear heart. Now a new door was opening.

By honoring and loving the past, you can release it and make room for the new. To see the past through the lens of love is a gift to your future. It allows you to create afresh. When you can freely greet the present moment with new eyes, the first lines of your new chapter can finally begin to write themselves.

 Exercise: *Write a Love Letter to Your Past*

What in your past is still lingering in the shadows? What transition are you finding yourself in? What is the dream that died?

You may be surprised by what comes up. You may feel that you had already let it go and healed it. Be compassionate with yourself and just notice the story you are still telling. This will reveal what is ready for your compassion to "come-pass-on."

What are you ready to put behind you—to complete? It might be a relationship to an ex-spouse or lover or boss, or a parent or sibling. It could be the ending of a job or career.

If you have difficulty recalling the good moments, journal about whatever is coming up first, with the intention of dumping your emotions on the page to get them out. Let yourself release any anger, sadness, despair, or feelings of betrayal. This will clear a space to remember and celebrate the positive aspects.

Writing a love letter to your past is a life-giving exercise that will powerfully move you forward. I suggest that you clear a couple of hours in your schedule. Light a candle and put on some music that feels nourishing. See this letter-writing activity as a self-loving ritual that will help your release anything in your past that you are still hanging on to.

You are about to free yourself.

Part I:

Allow yourself to remember everything positive about the past that you are releasing. Include the sensual, delicious, magical, expansive, or in-love moments. If there is a specific person or people involved, write the letter to that person or people.

Part II:

Ask a trusted friend, coach or counselor to witness your words as you read your letter aloud. Read your letter to someone your trust—someone who will honor the feelings and love expressed in your writing.

Important: Do not read or send the letter to the recipient unless you sense that it is safe to do so. Your wise inner guidance will tell you.

Got to Get You into My Life

We are human. No matter how spiritually oriented we are, we still have human desires. Some of these desires are more like essential needs. On each level of body, mind, and spirit, we need to be nourished. We all need to feel a sense of belonging to feel safe. To thrive, we need to feel loved.

But sometimes we get so fixated on wanting love to show up in a certain way that we close ourselves off from receiving it in any form. You may even, as I did, expect that your heart's desire will come in a specific package, like a tall, dark and handsome, sexy, spiritually evolved, masculine man who loves to dance, doesn't snore, and naturally intuits what makes you happy. Okay, I'm joking about the last part, but you get the idea.

The good news is that you can attract the *essence* of your desire in many different forms. In other words, you can't always get what you want, but you don't have to wait to get what you need.

For example, you may think it's the perfect-for-me man or woman you desire. Underneath this desire is what you want to *experience or feel* in the relationship. The experience—the feeling—is the essence. This underlying essence is the reason for the original desire in the first place. You only want something because you sense it will provide an opportunity to experience life and express yourself in a specific way—a way that will feel fantastic!

In moments of deep despair and loneliness, I wondered if my desire for a partner was just a cruel joke on the part of the Universe. What if this longing would never be fulfilled? I realize now that I was seeing myself as the victim of an incredibly unfair fate. I was afraid that the creator might have the key to some destiny I was not privy to. I certainly was not seeing myself as the generator of my own life experience!

Now I see it differently.

We live in a benevolent, unconditionally loving Universe that is absolutely supporting us to co-create our most cherished visions and dreams. But the Universe can only bestow the love and abundant blessings we seek if 1) we perceive it as loving and infinitely abundant, and 2) we are open to our desires showing up in ways we might not have imagined. In other words, what we do not see as possible we cannot receive.

In my own life, I had to ask myself a crucial question. If my partner had not yet shown up—and he obviously hadn't—what was the *essence* of what I desired? How could I satisfy my heart without the thing my heart wanted most?

I made a list of what I so wanted to experience with a life partner:

- Loving touch and affection
- Soulful companionship
- Dancing!
- Celebrating together with delicious food and drink
- Adventure and world travel
- The security of knowing that no matter what happens, we have each other's back

And here's the rub: I knew that if I was depriving myself of any of the things I desired to enjoy with my partner, I was the one kinking the hose. Spiritual law holds that we cannot receive from another person that which we are not giving ourselves. As I looked at the list, I asked myself, Is there anything here that I am not giving myself?

Again, being honest, I saw that I had been holing up too much at home, isolating myself. I was so focused on creating success in my work that I would avoid making advance social plans. I wasn't fully showing up for me.

I started with a simple request. I wrote to Spirit, asking my divine guidance to show me how to have more fun and bring me more opportunities to play. I knew I had to do my part as well. I returned to the essence of my desire to be with a life partner. What on that list could I say yes to now? I love to dance, so I committed to going out dancing more often. When I didn't have a friend to go with, I put on music and let loose at home.

I set the intention to meet more companions who resonated with values similar to mine. I made more dinner plans with these new friends. I also made a list of soul friends who truly *did* have my back, and began voicing my appreciation for their caring.

All this focused intention-setting worked. Love began to flow in—albeit in a completely different wrapping than I had envisioned.

Within a few days more love and support showed up. I serendipitously found a small business owner's support group and met my dear mentor and business coach, James Dunn. James not only inspired me with stories of adventurous personal and business risks he had taken, he also shared a similar spiritual perspective that inspired respect and trust. I also met a gifted massage therapist with whom I began trading coaching for massage, which helped meet my need for nurturing touch.

Whatever basic need or deep heart's desire you may be doing without, I want to encourage you to take a stand to get this into your life—in some form. I have deep compassion for wanting it to land on your doorstep, express delivery, in a specific package, believe me. But if your special order has not yet shown up, think of this next exercise as a healing bridge to receiving your envisioned desire.

Exercise: *Take a Stand for Your Life*

The essence of love eluded me, partly because I wasn't playing enough. I needed to have more fun and make plans with loving, like-minded friends. It was time to take a stand for my well-being—to leave my comfortable routine and seek more nourishing waters.

Now you:

Take a breath, relax, and reflect for a moment. Tune into what feels missing from your life. What important need is not being met? In this moment, what does your heart desire most?

Connect to the essence of what you want. The essence is what you imagine feeling, experiencing, expressing, and contributing through your heart's desire. For example, the essence of my desire for a life partner includes love, support, affection, adventurous travel, laughter, and dancing. What do you want to *feel* as a result of manifesting your desire?

Looking at what you wrote above, describe the essence of your desire …

Now reflect on what you might do differently to bring in your desire's essence.

- The one area of my life that absolutely needs to change is . . .

- Upon reflection, I can see that it's time to stop/start . . .

- To take care of my basic need for _____ (for example, affection and touch), I am willing to . . .

Write your stand for your life here. State your stand in the affirmative, present tense, as though you are already doing it. For example: I place my happiness and well-being first, before all else.

- My stand is . . .

Now choose one small step that furthers your stand in a practical way. In other words, make sure your small step will give you the essence of your desire. For example, "I dance and sing to one song daily in front of the mirror so I can feel and see my own joy."

- The one small step I will take toward living my stand is . . .

The Beauty of Giving Up

There's no substitute for knowing what makes your heart sing. Sometimes you're doing all the "right" things. You *are* doing "the work." You're jumping through all the spiritual hoops—meditating, praying, journaling, and writing to Spirit. You are visualizing the perfect-for-you partner by your side, feeling the wonderful sensations of having him or her near. Or you're imagining yourself in your dream career. Or seeing yourself vital and alive in radiant health. You're doing it all, and yet your heart's desire is still eluding you.

If you can relate to this, some part of you may still feel very much alone. This may feel like a last ditch effort. In truth, it is a golden opportunity. You are finally ready to let go of doing this journey on your own.

In my case, when, despite the prayers and requests and visioning, my loving partner still eluded me, I got mad. The on-my-knees-pounding-the-floor-in-tears kind of mad. I was feeling completely frustrated and out of answers for any other way to do my life. I finally surrendered all the way, even more than before, shouting, "I can't do this alone!" I basically sent out a deep cry. "Help! I need you! I see where this is going, and it's not going well. Show me another way!"

Very emphatically, I pleaded with Spirit to make its presence more deeply known to me. I took my prayers and communications to the next level. I started talking *out loud* to the creator. I found freeway driving to be a particularly good venue for heart-to-heart talks with the Divine. No one could hear me so I could be particularly animated without having to explain myself to anyone.

"Please, Spirit, let me *feel* you." I would raise my voice while driving and say, "I am in pain here. I am not doing this alone! I have tried it alone for years, and it's not working! You can see it's not working. I need your help! I need to know you have a reason for not bringing me my soul mate just now. I need to know what's going on. I need to *feel* you!"

I can't say that I received clear answers right away, but the process of giving up and giving in to Spirit made me feel a new level of calm. Like a three-year-old having a tantrum who finally lets go and cries herself to sleep, I, or I should say my ego, was finally ready to hand it over.

I could feel that I was on to something. The more I spoke out loud to Spirit, voicing my sometimes overwhelming emotions, the less I felt alone, and the more I felt connected to my inner guidance. I was finally ready to stop trying so diligently to make my desires happen. I was ready, more than ready, to partner with Spirit and hand over the reins to my life so I wouldn't have to work so hard.

I threw in the towel. The last, tattered shred of my resistance to knowing that I was truly and safely anchored in the Divine—I handed it over to Spirit.

And a deeper faith took root.

Even now I am surprised that ranting and raving to Spirit would be the ticket. It made our bond feel more real—until it *became* real. Until *I* became real.

You can seek security outside of yourself in a partner or job, but it's an illusion that anything outside of you can give you *true* security. Your essential rootedness can only be found in your connection to your own spirit, to the Creator, to that to which you are spiritually tethered. This connection is not only eternal, it is wired into your being, like a direct line to the Divine.

 Practice: *Freeway Prayers*

If, like me, you are ready to take your connection to Spirit to the next level, try this: talk to your higher power *out loud.*

Feel free to put it all out there! Get mad, cry, scream, shout, or celebrate with glee. Let your emotions have a voice. Pour your heart out to your unconditionally loving soul partner.

Are you ready to give your soul the reins to your life? If so, say so. Voicing your thoughts, feelings and prayers magnifies the power of your words. Sound adds a heightened dimension to our intention, and sends the vibration of your truth out into the airwaves.

I encourage you to keep track of your rants, raves, and other conversations with your Divine Beloved in your journal. Notice how your connection deepens when you take this step to make your bond more real.

Opening to a New Vision

I was beginning to feel the love of my soul more deeply than ever before. The longing I had felt for a soul mate partner was being satisfied by tending to my own soul. I was finally giving myself the love I wanted to experience with a companion and husband. I still wanted to meet a life partner—I wasn't giving up on manifesting that desire. But I was ready to acknowledge that if he didn't show up, I could still create a beautiful life for myself. This was a huge breakthrough! I was finally ready to imagine an alternate possibility and open to a new vision.

I asked myself, If a partner is not part of my immediate future, what would I love to do, be, and have in my life? Since my sweetheart isn't here yet, where am I being called?

For more than a year, I had felt my soul nudging me to write a book. A book about all I had learned since I'd begun searching for my passionate right livelihood. It was time to answer this call—to give practical wings to my creativity and share my experiences in writing.

I committed. And then I began procrastinating. In the past, I have been especially gifted at turning any genuinely inspired project into drudgery. I can be over-the-moon excited with an idea, but when I sit down to focus on it, I feel as though a heavy weight has been laid on my shoulders.

I remember my dad telling me as a kid to "stop lollygagging around" (translation: stop dreaming) and "get to work." In other words, work is a serious responsibility. Built into this is a belief that work makes you miserable. Needless to say, this inner wiring takes the lightness and fun out of any creation.

Consciously I was firmly committed to writing the book, but some unconscious part of me wasn't fully on board. I began to write and then felt lonely again. Like my workshop prep and newsletter writing, this was another solitary project. I desired companionship—soulful companionship. The part of me that wanted partnership wanted collaboration in my writing as well. The book wasn't flowing. So I wrote to Spirit again:

Dear Spirit,

Here I am and it's time to write my book, and I'm in that waffling place again. I am ready to surrender. I want you, my soul, to come in fully and take over.

I want to give you the reins to my life. Please guide me, Spirit. Please remind me that I'm partnering with you as the voice of my soul in writing this book. That the small "I" isn't writing the book, the big "I AM" is writing the book.

I want to see you as my deep soul partner in creativity. Not just as a muse, so to speak, but I need to feel that you and I are writing this together. That we are pairing up. You tell me, please. I am open and ready. And I will feel so much better knowing that we are a team with deep, abiding love for each other.

Love,
Betsy

And Spirit replied …

Beloved, of course, this is our adventure together! Together we are guiding others to let go of the fears, doubt, and worry as they've "practiced" them. But not just that. We—you and I—are to become wedded to one another in this process. In the process of writing this book, you and I are becoming ONE.

Me: *So it's okay to make this book the bridge to a deeper knowing. A knowing that not only are we connected, but that it's safe to give you the reins to my life?*

Spirit: *Yes! Yes! Yes! I am going to guide you on the path to crossing this bridge to oneness. I'll be guiding you every step of the way. Together we'll have a delicious time and romp through the woods of joy and wild abandon of knowing. How is that?*

Me: *That is great! I'm mostly in—what do I need to do to get more in?*

Spirit: *Ha, ha, ha, my love. I'll be pulling you in as we go. Ours is an affair of the heart. We will journey together, having fun and passionate exchanges along the way. The key is letting go and surrendering to our union. We are partnering! We are having a soul union. We'll be making it all up—creating it—as we go along.*

I felt another whoosh of yes! My conscious dialogue with Spirit blew in a new wind beneath my wings. I felt a brand new enthusiasm bubble up. After our sweet and loving exchange, I felt high. Sitting in my neighborhood Peet's Coffee & Tea shop, I wanted to shout to the friendly baristas, "Guess what, I had a breakthrough! I'm not writing this book *alone*. I am partnering with my soul—we're doing it together! Doesn't that rock?!"

 Exercise: *Team Up with Spirit*

Now you:

What would you say yes to if you knew you had all the support you needed to succeed with flying colors?

If I had all the time, money, contacts, and resources I needed, I would say *yes* to …

Ask your spiritual source for everything you need to move forward. On the following page, write a note to Spirit, or whatever you call you inner wise guidance. Reveal to your loving soul exactly what your heart most desires. Write it out in as much detail as you can. It can be a tiny action step or a big vision. Spirit doesn't care how big or small it is.

Ask for all the reassurance that you need, as I did in the example to the left. I often dialogue with Spirit for pages. We go back and forth until I feel at peace and supported with the comfort and answers I need to move forward.

Write a note to Spirit ...

Now write an answer back from Spirit to you ...

5

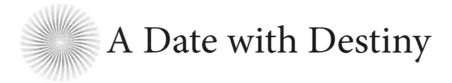

A Date with Destiny

Stuff your eyes with wonder; live as if you'd drop dead in ten seconds. See the world. It's more fantastic than any dream made or paid for in factories.

~ Ray Bradbury

There is a grand and gorgeous mystery to this life. Open your heart and ask for the miraculous to touch you.

~ A Journal Entry

I wish I had known from an early age that the Universe is conspiring to make our desires reality. I wish I had learned that all we need is an inspired idea and the Universe will join with us to bring its essence into being. That each of us comes to life with a heroic purpose that only *we* can accomplish—our unique destiny—a destiny that the world needs whether we know it or not. And that our presence here is so important and needed, we can rely on a force greater than ourselves to support our glorious unfolding. We can count on this divine assistance to carry us into the vision of fully becoming who we are meant to be.

I wish I had known, too, that sometimes, when it feels like nothing is happening, you need to stop waiting and take action. You need to release your attachment to the idea that your heart's desire must look a certain way. This is wonderfully empowering because you are taking charge of your destiny. You are consciously choosing to generate your own happiness. This has the effect of loosening rigid thinking and shaking up your routine in a life-giving way.

A little shaking up of life is a good thing. When you feel stuck, you need to move. The soul loves adventure, and you absolutely need it to thrive.

I've always had a dream to travel the world. My sense is that we live on a vast and magnificent planet of infinite beauty. I don't know if I can experience all the gorgeous places of this incredible world in one lifetime, but I wouldn't mind trying! From the beginning of my healing arts career, I had enthusiastically imagined myself touring the globe, speaking, writing, and giving workshops about saying yes to your heart.

Once Spirit and I made a pact to write the book together, I began feeling a strong nudge to get on a plane and go someplace warm. Images of a healing oasis—a tropical beach and sun on my body—flooded in. My wandering heart was calling. I needed to give myself an adventure. I had an exciting idea: what if I took a trip to a scenically beautiful country and worked on my book in a new, inspiring place? What if I gifted myself with a self-created writing retreat?

Don't Wait for Your Birthday

After I made the decision to take a stand for my life, to stop waiting for my life partner to show up, and, instead, to give myself what I desire, I noticed a real shift. My self-care routine was working. I was dancing more, laughing more, and feeling lighter and happier. I decided to make my writing vacation feel as abundant as possible. I eagerly anticipated a productive *and* delicious trip during which I would make lots of progress on my book and be nourished with ample sun, swimming in the warm ocean, and feeling the sweet, balmy breeze on my skin.

I reserved a beautiful condominium in the old town of Puerto Vallarta, also known as the "romantic zone," a few blocks from the ocean in a lovely compound called Selva Romantica. Just hearing the name of the place lit me up. "I'll be staying at Selva Romantica," I delighted in sharing with a few close friends. "Oh, you're going to have a romance!" everyone remarked immediately. "Really ... do you think so?!" I responded. The prospect felt wonderful. "Sounds fun," I would say, laughing. "But no,

I am going to work on my book." I even consulted the owner of the condo specifically about my purpose. He assured me that the open air living area with a lush hillside view would be a perfect place to write.

As soon as I stepped into my penthouse Mexican oasis, I was practically screaming with joy. *Everything about this place is perfect!* I thought. Exhausted from being up since 3:30 a.m. the night before, I walked in to see the charming mahogany-and-glass French doors opened wide to let in the sweet-and-spicy floral scented air. I felt as if the place itself was welcoming me home. Visions of angels were everywhere: folk art angels hung over my bed; dreamy angels floating in heaven were painted on the living room hutch. My guardian angels and a hand-painted wood block painting of goddess Mother Mary in my writing area made me feel lovingly watched over and guided. My home-away-from-home couldn't have been more perfect if I had custom-designed it myself. My body buzzed with the excitement of these affirming synchronicities.

All around the complex were winding stone pathways lined with tropical flowers in pinks, yellows, oranges, fuchsias, and reds. I must have taken a hundred photos of the gardens alone on my first day. I was completely enamored with the stunning beauty all around me.

The first thing I did upon awakening each morning was open up all the glass doors and consciously breathe in the succulent fragrances. *Yesss!* I celebrated inwardly. I sat quietly and felt my heart open wide as I watched the sun rise over the emerald green mountainside dotted with red-tile roofs. *I am so happy to be here,* I kept feeling, deep appreciation coursing through my bones. I would reach for the sky, stretch, and thank Spirit for delivering this gift to me. *Thank you, thank you, thank you! I am so blessed!*

I felt this gratitude in every cell of my body. My trusted confidante Doris had told me several months earlier, "I am getting the sense that you need heat." Her words came back to me. *Yes! I am getting the warmth I need!*

I would then make my way into my beautiful little Mexican-tiled kitchen to steam milk for a Latin latte on the fancy Italian espresso-maker. I loved the taste of the local beans. I couldn't have been more in heaven.

Of course *I* had given this gift to *me*. This was not my usual way. In the past, I might have settled for lesser accommodations. But I had a clear intention to make headway on my writing, and being sensitive to my environment, I knew I needed both quiet and beauty to feel at home in my surroundings.

I was taking really good care of myself, and the Universe was responding in kind.

In the past, I had been generous with everyone but me. I grew up thinking that giving to others was the way to be a "good person." As a mom, friend, worker, and wife, I would give ninety-eight percent of my energy to others, assuming I would receive the same in return. When my hopes or expectations were dashed, I would end up feeling disappointed or resentful. I didn't understand why I wasn't getting back what I was giving.

I remember one birthday in my early twenties, when my ex-husband and I wandered into a silver jewelry store on the beautiful island of Martha's Vineyard. The island's quaint beauty inspired my romantic heart. I showed him a pair of inexpensive, yet uniquely designed fish-shaped earrings that caught my eye. He admired them but didn't take my nudge. I later felt sad and let down that he didn't respond to my not-so-subtle hint. Upon reflection, I was simply playing out the inner belief that *I can't have what I want.* If anyone was going to change this pattern, it had to be me.

When he and I parted, I resolved to be more generous with myself. Instead of waiting for my birthday or Christmas, I decided to be more proactive and say yes to my desires—within my budget—more often. One day, I happened upon a half-price clearance sale on freshwater pearl-and-crystal bead necklaces. I made a bold move: I bought myself not just one but three of the necklaces. It was a daring action for me, but I see now what a good move it was.

Going out of my normal mode to give myself more than my inner, stingy critic said that I needed sent a strong message to my subconscious mind:

I am worth treating myself like a precious heirloom.

In my experience, if you want to have something more or different from what you've been getting, you have to be open to receiving more. As my spiritual counselor, Jan, once asked me, "How much are you willing to receive, Betsy? How large is your container?"

The Universe can only fill a space as wide as you're opening your arms to embrace.

Every time I go out of my comfort zone to treat myself especially well, my ego rebels. I've come to recognize this as part of the process of saying yes to a bigger container. I know that when I treat myself as generously as I want the Universe to treat me, the powerful cosmic forces cannot help but respond in kind.

 Exercise: *Open to Receive Something Wonderful*

Everything you've ever experienced began in your imagination, even the situations you didn't invite. Since you can only create what you first imagine, take a moment to let your inner magician enter your heart.

What if you could wave a magic wand and materialize whatever your heart desires? Take a moment to relax and play with this possibility. Allow yourself to imagine something wonderful coming into your life.

Step 1:

Write down three experiences, conditions, or things that you would love to receive.

If answers don't come immediately, spend a few moments getting quiet, taking in a few deep breaths, and relaxing first. Then complete the following questions:

- The most joyful thing that could happen to me is …

- The most delightful experience I can imagine creating is …

- I would be thrilled to announce the celebration of …

Step 2:

Go back and look at each answer, one at a time. What about this description lights you up?

For example, I love sparkling, colorful jewelry because I love beauty, art, and nature's creations. Wearing something pretty makes me feel beautiful.

Write down next to each answer what you believe it will give you. This is the essence of your desire. Do you notice a common theme around what lights you up?

Step 3:

How might you give this essence to yourself? Just for fun, open your mind and heart to other possibilities. How could you experience this essence now? Is there one thing you can do to be more generous with yourself?

Write it down …

A Magnet for Unexpected Magic

I was so in love with my Mexican condominium's beauty—and so thrilled to be experiencing this exotic, sunny writing adventure—that my happiness put me into a flow of joyful appreciation for everything new and beautiful I encountered.

What I know for sure is that the times in my life when I've received unexpected blessings like this, my heart was open and ready. I believed that something new, different, and serendipitously fun and delicious could happen. And I wasn't attached to the outcome. If what I desired didn't happen, so be it. I felt relaxed about my request. I threw out my desire in a playful way, almost as if I was flirting with the Universe.

In these seemingly magical moments, we are "in the vortex," as Abraham-Hicks calls the powerful place of being magnetic to our desires.[8] According to the Law of Attraction, your thoughts and feelings radiate a signal, also known as a vibrational frequency.[9] When you are feeling the positive emotions associated with obtaining your desires, you radiate a vibrational frequency that the Law of Attraction must match. In the vortex, you vibrate at the frequency of your intention, which means that you can easily draw your heart's desire to you like a magnet.

In other words, everything is made of energy, including you. Thus, you are always emitting a specific energetic vibration. Like radio waves, you send out a signal that reflects your consciousness of the moment. You attract your desire when your vibrational frequency, or signal, is a match to the frequency of your desire.

As you might guess, depression has a very low frequency. In contrast, appreciation, gratitude, and love each have a high frequency. I found myself in this beautiful place, walking around in a state of overflowing joy, loving everything I saw. I felt "in the zone," as we say, feeling completely grateful for the gift of Puerto Vallarta.

Experiencing these "higher-altitude" emotions makes you a powerful magnetic attractor. Being in a state of appreciation and gratitude is a *yes* state of mind.

You are now seeing through a whole new lens—a lens of infinite possibility. In this state, your heart is open to receiving. Now in the flow, you have all the necessary conditions to be guided by your soul. You are in the perfect position, as you send out your intention, to receive insights and direction on the actions that will bring your desire to fruition.

Perhaps this is why, on my first night in Mexico, my spirit led me directly to something I had been praying for and wanting with all my heart.

I was feeling so in love with Vallarta that I didn't let the news of a forecasted hurricane—and almost certain power outage—deter me from enjoying myself. I had traveled all day to be in the warm tropical air. The sky grew dark and it started to rain, then thunder, with flashes of lightning. I know people say this is dangerous for swimming, but my intuition said a quick dip would be safe. What better place to be than swimming in the salt-water infinity pool and taking in the expansive ocean view?

The very first person I met at the pool was a lady whose birthday happened to be on the exact same day as mine. Like me, she would be celebrating her special day in Mexico that week. Whenever statistically unlikely things like this happen—synchronicities and serendipities—it's always a good sign that we're in the flow.

After my swim, the rain stopped so I ventured out for dinner. It was dark, the old cobblestoned streets were dotted with potholes filled with mud puddles, and I had no idea where I was going. I also know almost no Spanish. "Spirit, lead me!" I asked, as I so often do when I find myself in new territory. I had only been to Vallarta one other time, eleven years earlier on a trip with my former husband. We had stayed in the busy hotel zone but we discovered the old town toward the end of our trip. Loving the old-world charm of Viejo Vallarta, I had noted that if we ever returned, I would definitely want to stay here.

On the last night of the trip with my husband, we were drawn in by beautiful music coming from a lovely beachfront restaurant called La Brisa. With the warm ocean breeze flowing into the simply elegant candle-lit lounge, we listened to Miguel, a soulful guitarist sing passionate ballads that moved my heart all evening. We wanted to take his CD home with us, but he had sold out that evening. He very generously offered to deliver one to our hotel the next morning since we were returning to Seattle that day. When my husband and I split up our music collection, I was the recipient of Miguel's CD. I had been listening to his music, on and off, for the past decade.

Many years had passed since I'd been there, and it was hard to find my way in the dark. Still, I felt safe and guided. My friends from the pool waved me down and said hello, inviting me to join them for dinner. They were friendly and kind, but smoking cigarettes, which deterred me. My intuition said to keep walking. Moments later, I found myself standing right in front of La Brisa!

I had only met Miguel that one time, and very briefly, to ask about his CD, but seeing him again eleven years later made my heart warm. He was still playing guitar and his voice sounded just the same, velvety smooth and soulful. The waiters went out of their way to make me feel comfortable. They even hung my rain slicker on a portable coat rack they brought over just for my table. I'd never seen such a gesture in the United States. It made me smile. I felt like I was home.

When the last set was over, Miguel, a dark and handsome man, greeted me warmly. Though I had barely met him all those years earlier, I felt instantly at ease with him. Also an accomplished painter, he and I easily fell into talking about our passions and what made us happy. We both expressed our love for music, beauty, and art, and how we wanted to grow and express more freely in our creative lives.

We soon realized that we both had daughters, that two of his girls were close in age to my two, and that we were now both divorced. And then Miguel said something that struck a deep chord within me. "I have been divorced for four years now," he offered. "My heart is healed. I am now finally at peace with being alone."

Wow! I thought, he took the words right out of my heart. After struggling for so long with *when will my soul mate finally show up?* I had let go and decided to be happy no matter what. I had resolved to love my life, and myself, solo or partnered. Like Miguel, I finally felt at peace with being alone.

And now, on my very first evening in magical Puerto Vallarta, I was meeting a man who seemed to speak my same language. I had no idea where our relationship was going beyond this, but I did know that in talking with Miguel, I felt the soulful companionship I had been asking for. "Thank you, Universe! Thank you, my dear soul," I exclaimed inside, "for this beautiful gift."

The Magic of Being Present

I've often noticed that vacations can seem so much more wonderful than what we call "real" life. This is partly because we are on holiday from our work routines. As well, we are in new territory, so we must pay attention. Finding our way around requires our full presence or we may get lost.

In Vallarta, for example, the old town was mostly brand new to me. Everything I saw was like walking into a beautiful scene in a movie I was seeing for the very first time. Since I didn't know how to get to the beach, La Brisa, or the local bus stop, my senses were on high alert.

When all of your senses are fully activated, you are completely and utterly present. You feel much more alive and open. Being open and present is like turning on the lights for the very first time in a gorgeously decorated room. Or seeing a sweet nuance in your longtime lover's face, one that you've never before noticed.

You are more likely to experience the soul qualities of appreciation, joy, beauty, and love while on holiday because you are in the higher, more magnetic frequency of being in the now. Being present elevates you to this higher vibrational frequency. Words like on *top of the world* and *walking on air* describe the feeling. I call it being in the *love flow*, because you're experiencing life in the higher altitudes. You are connected to and swimming in your soul's natural essence of pure love.

Intention plays into high-altitude living as well. You usually decide before you go away on vacation that you're going to have a wonderful time. Decisions are commitments, and commitments are powerful. They tell the subconscious mind how to direct energy. Few of us set the same intention for our everyday work lives. It's very easy to get stuck in a rut of seeing work through the lens of routine, obligation, or drudgery. You may love your paycheck but frame your job as a necessary chore to get what you need.

But what if you saw your routine, instead, as a joyful enterprise in living? What if you had the same intention each and every day—weekday, workday, play day, or weekend day—that today is going to be a fantastic day?!

Every soul shares the same deep desire for more—more passion, more fulfillment, more meaning. We all want to feel freer to experience more joy, inner peace, and bliss, all the time, not just on our "time off." That we even call our nonwork time *time off* bears some reflection.

When I was in Puerto Vallarta, I noticed travelers who were heading back home say the phrase *back to reality* in a resigned and dejected tone. It was as though they were held captive by a less-than-satisfying life at home. In truth, they were leaving their vacation state of mind and entering their everyday-reality state of mind. Clearly, the first mindset is more life-affirming, but we are often not conscious that *we* are the ones who create our mindsets! We are also the ones who decide that work time is going to feel less wonderful than time off, and perhaps as heavy as drudgery.

You might say that you haven't created this idea—that your work *is* stressful or dull, or that your boss or coworkers truly make your work difficult to enjoy. You might feel that you have no choice but to feel unhappy or unfulfilled at work. If you are feeling this way, I encourage you to at least claim your power. Wherever you are, you always have a choice, even if you're choosing not to recognize it!

Acknowledge that you are choosing this for now, but that you are not a victim of your circumstances. Maybe you're looking for another job but haven't received any offers, so you think you're trapped. The ego sees life in black and white, either/or, yes or no. For example, you might say, "Either I keep my job or I lose my home." But in truth, there are many other possibilities in between, including getting a roommate, staying with a relative, or moving to a less expensive home. These options may not be desirable to you, and honoring your values is important. It is helpful, however, to open up space in your mind and remember that as residents of this infinite universe, we always have alternatives available to us.

In contrast to feeling stuck, a much more freeing way to look at life is *I don't have to stay here if I don't want to. Just for right now I am choosing to stay, but I can change my mind in any moment. I always have options, even if I don't know at this moment what they are.*

Whatever you are receiving that is keeping you where you are is a gift. This can be a source of gratitude for you. You can choose to feel grateful that your work is serving this important purpose for you. Rather than feeling victimized by having to stay where you don't want to be, become aware that you are, in fact, making a choice to remain there because it is satisfying something you need right now, such as a paycheck. This will bring you a new surge of power and let you take back your birthright to feel happy no matter what.

Being present is a practice. You leave and go into the future or the past in your mind, and come back to the now. The goal is always the same: to return to the *love flow*. To reconnect with your soul and check in with your heart: How am I feeling right now? What do I need? Everything you need to know, your heart can tell you. Your heart has your divine prescription in any given moment.

The following exercise will connect you to your soul's inner wisdom and help you reframe any situation that may be taking you out of your love flow. You free yourself when you shift to seeing with new eyes.

✳ **Exercise:** *Sing Praises for What Is*

Part I:

Become aware of a person, situation, or condition in your life that is causing you to feel stressed or trapped.

Name it, such as: I hate my job. Or, I'm having difficulties in my marriage.

Next, reflect on the benefits the situation or relationship is giving you. What do you appreciate about it? Write down every thing you can think of, beginning with the tiniest thing. If you can't think of anything, it means that the stress, anger, sadness, anxiety, or fear you are feeling needs a voice first.

Right now I am feeling …

Now that you've named and dumped your emotions on the page, come back to the benefits.

Here are a few examples:

My house is giving me a safe place to live.

My body may be ill, but I can still walk.

My spouse is driving me crazy, but I appreciate that s/he cooks meals for us.

The benefit(s) of my current situation include …

Part II:

Keep a gratitude list.

As you shift your focus from the negatives of life to the gifts of being alive, looking for all the things your current life is giving you, you free yourself. I encourage you to begin a daily practice of writing a list of things you are grateful for. Especially on the more challenging days, you may feel a lot of resistance to making your list. Do it anyway. Begin with simple things like your ability to walk, feel the sunlight, or appreciate a full moon. Do your best to appreciate something about where you are. If you do this, your job, relationship, or whatever isn't fulfilling you, will either become more enjoyable or it will be replaced with a better opportunity. Gratitude always raises your vibration so you can attract the next best situation.

I am grateful for …

Nourishing Your Soul

It is true that on vacation we give ourselves more freedom than we generally have in our regular routine, when we are on a schedule of predetermined hours. Even if you are self-employed and create your own schedule, you still have to show up for appointments and commitments you've made. When you're on holiday, by contrast, it feels wonderful to wake up and know that you are totally flexible and can do anything you want. You are free to respond to all that life is broadcasting and offering in the moment. You are free to change your mind. You can do something else or nothing at all, whenever you choose.

When you feel this free, you are totally open, and a new sense of possibility comes into your consciousness. A new sense of spaciousness comes into your being, which is like a wonderful whoosh of fresh air. Especially if you've been feeling stressed, cramped, trapped or overloaded, it feels absolutely sublime. It's the feeling of *Ah … now I have room to breathe!*

You may even begin to contemplate other ways to do your life so that you can feel more of this spaciousness, more of the time. You drop your guard and let the fullness of life enter your heart and mind. What's happening is that you are opening the door to experience the fullness of yourself—your *true* self. You are feeling more alive because you are connecting to your soul's essence of pure love. This love is so full of light, it feels warm and full and delicious. No wonder you want to stay here and never go "back to reality!"

The soul needs a free block of time, so that you can fully experience its fullness through the freedom of an unstructured stretch of time. Time to put aside your responsibilities, places you have to be, and things you have to do. Time to unplug, silence the phone, be in wonder, let the mind wander, and linger freely in awe. In this space, you finally give yourself room to pause, breathe, relax, and just experience life without any preconceived notions of what you need to do or accomplish.

Your soul as the essence of love wants to have this deeper and fuller connection with you. Your soul is like a lover, asking you for a date night.

Even if you don't yet fully trust that your soul is full of love for you, think of it this way: your soul is your creative soul mate—your inner muse. It has something *you* desire: connection to the clarity, confidence, calm, and courage that you seek.

When you take the time out to make a date with your soul, the rewards you reap run deep. The emptiness, restlessness, angst, or sorrow begins to transform. When you create space to hear the voice of your soul, your inspiration, your wise guidance, has a chance to come through. You connect with your truth. You begin to sense more of who you really are. You've opened the channels of love.

Make a Date with Your Destiny

When I ask my clients to begin taking weekly Soul Dates, I notice a similar response. They've signed on to transform their lives, so they *are* eager and game to try new things. They've tried a lot of other things that haven't worked, so they are generally very open to changing things up … at least a bit. For sure, they are very ready to experience a shift, a breath of fresh air and clarity—and as soon as possible, of course.

However, this assignment often brings the biggest ego pushback. The resistance is palpable. Commonly, I see a blank look, which turns to a trepidation-filled yet polite response, such as, "O-ka-a-a-y, well, I'm willing to tr-r-r-r-y-y-y it. From their response, you would think that I casually asked them to venture downtown and dance naked across the most congested, major city intersection in the dead of winter.

The Soul Date brings up resistance because the ego doesn't want to be left alone with itself. It fears an open-ended space of time. It wants a schedule. It wants to know exactly where it's going and what it will see and when it will be home, kind of like a scared child who doesn't want their mommy to go out for an evening with friends.

I remember my first Soul Date. I did my best to stay open. I wanted to hear the voice of my spirit's direction, so I didn't make an advance plan beyond carving out a three-hour time block in my appointment book. At the appointed time, I drove out of my driveway and asked my inner guide, "Okay, where are we going?" I got a nudge to go to Archie McPhee's, a toy store that caters to adults as much as little kids. This active, happy place is full to the brim with colorful wind-up toys and little plastic figures, Hawaiian leis, sparkly Happy Birthday banners, and kites strung up all over the ceiling. I let myself wander the store and explore like a five-year-old, winding up the little toys and watching them move and dance, just because I could. It was exactly what I needed—to play!

And this is why Soul Dates work: our spirit knows exactly what kind of nourishment we need in any moment.

When carried out with an open, curious mind and a consciously-made invitation to Spirit, your Soul Dates will lead you to treasures that inform your path and move you forward. The key is to be light and playful about them. Don't put a lot of pressure for any one Soul Date to reveal the blueprint of your destiny. Like any intention, you want to put it out there and then release your attachment to a specific outcome. Stay present, let yourself be spontaneous, and enjoy each moment—whatever it brings.

Here's the assignment: go on a solo excursion that feeds your soul. Preferably once a week, for at least two to three hours (I prefer three). The goal is to create space for your inner guidance to show up. Your Soul Date can include anything from walking in the woods to browsing a beautiful artsy paper store to taking yourself out to that movie you've been wanting to see.

The only rule is *you can't take anyone with you*. Why? Because relating to a companion, while lovely, tends to take up the space for intentionally cultivating a partnership with your soul. The space you need to hear the quiet whispers of this wise self that knows the bigger plan of why you're here.

When you're wandering on your own, you feel freer. Freer to let something catch your eye and lead you to the next thing your delighted muse wants to show you. Your soul knows you like no companion ever could. It knows exactly what you need, when you need it. On a Soul Date, your unconditionally loving soul is charged with carrying out your intention. It dutifully shows up to spark the next idea or land you in the perfect place to get the nudge, sign, or synchronicity that leads you to the next place in your destiny. That is, if *you* show up.

My clients want to know what the difference is between a Soul Date and going out for fun. It's all in your intention. Soul Dates are for consciously creating space for you and your inspiration. Hence, they have a magical quality to them. You are going out looking for magic—to co-create magical possibility with your inner soul mate companion. The Universe, in turn, does its part to meet you halfway with delight. And often, with inspired direction.

One more thing: your ego will probably continue to throw up obstacles to following through on your Soul Dates. Keep them sacred like you would a date with a new significant other that you are crazy about. Resist the temptation to reschedule when someone else seems to desperately need your time. Remember that you have committed to receive the clarity, inspiration, and connection to your soul that you so desire. Soul Dates are non-negotiable. Saying yes to nurturing your relationship with your inner muse is you keeping your part of the bargain.

Now you:

Open your calendar and schedule in time for your Soul Date. Be generous with yourself. How much time do you need to relax, let go, and enjoy being guided by your soul? Block out what you need. Then invite your creative inner companion to give you nudges on where to go and what to do. And above all, have fun!

6

The Power of Support

Each friend represents the world in us, a world possibly not born until they arrive. And it is only by this meeting that a new world is born.

~ Anais Nin

Replace the outworn, unsupportive voices of the past with new, encouraging, and uplifting ones. True enthusiastic supporters can override the inner critics of doubt and fear that might otherwise keep you stuck. For every new dream, you need a tribe in which to birth it. Your tribe awaits your presence—they need you as much as you need them!

~ A Journal Entry

When I first imagined traveling to Puerto Vallarta, I envisioned writing with an inspiring view of the ocean. Maybe because I grew up near the beach, I always feel an expanded sense of possibility looking out over sun-sparkled, blue-green waters that seem to go on forever. But for this trip, oceanfront accommodations were beyond my budget. I had also heard that their location on the busy *Malecon*, or boardwalk, could be noisy in the evenings with so many vacationers out enjoying music and other festivities. So I gave up the ocean view for a peaceful location a bit inland.

Then, the day after my arrival, I shared photos on Facebook of all the gorgeous beauty I was encountering. A family friend, Brian, saw my post and encouraged me to get in touch with his dad, Ray. It turns out that Ray owns an oceanfront condominium in Puerto Vallarta that he wasn't using, just three blocks from my quiet accommodations. Ray generously offered it to me as my "sea-view writing office." Without any doing on my part, the Universe fulfilled my desire for both an inspired view by day and a peaceful sleep at night.

I was delighted by this gift, and once more felt validated in my knowing that the Universe provides in ways beyond our imagination, as this truly was beyond anything I had conceived of happening.

But there is even more to this story. As I mentioned earlier, my father, Gene Guy Gutting, passed away of a sudden heart attack at the young age of forty-nine. I was just sixteen. At the time, my parents were separated and my father was living in Santa Cruz, California, an eight-hour drive from our family home in Irvine.

Although my dad had a big heart and was a very passionate, loving man, he was from the old school of discipline and could be quite stern with his four daughters. As a result, we all felt afraid of our father at times. He could also be described as a workaholic, so even when he was living with us, he was often absent and I never felt that I knew him very well. In addition, in my adolescent and early teen years, my parents often fought in front of us, and I experienced my dad's words toward my mom as harsh. My mom would confide in me, complaining of my dad's preoccupation with his work as well as other problems in their marriage. I sided with my mom and unconsciously believed that it was my job to protect her. Because of this, my relationship with my dad was especially strained when my parents were separated, just before his death.

After he passed, I missed my father terribly and years later chose to consciously heal my relationship with him *in spirit*. I learned that although we shed our bodies at death, our souls are eternal, and we can continue to communicate with our departed loved ones, and even heal any differences we had with them before their passing.

One day, I heard a wise teacher remark, "in order to fulfill her purpose in the world and have a loving relationship with a man, a daughter needs to feel her father's blessing." She needs to know she is precious in his eyes. She needs to feel that she is lovable exactly the way she is. And that no matter what happens in her life, he has her back. This was a profound revelation for me. It dawned on me that I had never felt this from my father. At least in my own mind and heart, I had never received his blessing.

Over time, I practiced envisioning myself as a little girl, sitting on my father's lap as he stroked my hair and looked lovingly into my eyes, telling me how proud he was of me. This I could imagine my father doing, because even though I don't recall hearing such words from him directly, I do remember his work colleagues sharing at his end-of-life celebration how proud our dad was of his girls. These visualizations had a profound healing effect on me. I began to feel on a visceral level that my father loved me deeply.

When he passed, my mother, sisters, and I flew to Santa Cruz for his funeral service. I think I was still in shock from him leaving our lives so suddenly. Having to travel to attend his service made the whole event feel even more surreal. But when we arrived, one of my father's close friends, Ray, greeted all of us warmly and took us under his wing for the entire weekend. His four sons, including Brian, embraced us as if we were their sisters.

Fast forward to the present. Months before coming to Puerto Vallarta, I had been communicating with my dad in spirit. My dad was a brilliant entrepreneur, so I had been calling on him to help me grow a financially successful business. Now that I was committing to write my book, I asked him specifically for his help, both in material resources and inspiration. Daddy himself had always wanted to write a nonfiction book and was just beginning to do so when the heart attack took his life.

I don't know how our loved ones who have crossed over assist us in carrying out our dreams here on earth, I only sense that they do. This is part of the mystery of the invisible realm that we do not have access to.

It is one thing to intellectually know that we can continue our relationships with loved ones in spirit and receive their guidance, it is another to really *feel* it. I wanted to bridge the gap between knowing this in my mind and fully feeling my father's presence and support. So I put additional photos of him around my house to remind me that he is always with me. As I walked by a photo, I would stop and acknowledge him, send him love, and affirm, *I know you are with me. I am more than ready for your continued support! Please help me feel you with me.*

As a result, before coming to Vallarta, I was beginning to feel even closer to my dad.

Although we connected on Facebook a few years ago, it had been more than thirty years since I had seen Brian or Ray. When Brian nudged me, through Facebook, to call his dad and Ray offered me a writing haven overlooking the beach, I got a strong feeling that my dad had coordinated our contact. Most importantly, I felt as though my dad was connecting us to show me that he truly does have my back. That he is with me, cheering me on, and even coordinating practical assistance to support my endeavors.

This heavenly confirmation that Daddy was in fact supporting me was wonderfully healing for me. The experience was even more profound as I also witnessed the healing ripple out to others.

When I shared with Brian that I felt my dad was responsible for connecting us, he began to cry. Brian told me that the day my dad passed, he had been en route to play tennis with him. Daddy suffered a heart attack just before Brian arrived for their tennis date. Brian, who was only fourteen at the time, confided that he had always regretted not showing up earlier, thinking that maybe there was something he could have done to save his life.

I responded that Brian couldn't have done anything differently and shared my belief that passing when he did was, in the bigger picture, timed in accordance with my dad's divine destiny. I couldn't help but feel that another healing was happening for both of us. A healing that would not have occurred had I not shared my photos on Facebook, had Brian not seen my post, and had I not followed up by accepting Ray's invitation to use his condo for my writing.

In saying yes to my soul's urges along the way, we both received a powerful healing brought on by my father answering my prayers.

Brian also shared with me that he had loved my dad immensely. My dad was dating Brian's mom at the time he passed, and Daddy and Brian had become very close. For the first time, I was able to see my dad in a new light. Although he was not able to be there for me in ways that I would have wanted, he *had* been giving his love and support to Brian. Because I had consciously chosen to heal my relationship with my father over the years, I could now receive Brian's sharing with joy, rather than feeling that I had missed out on the fatherly love that he had received.

Finally, Brian added that my father had confided something else before he passed: that he was incredibly proud of his four beautiful daughters and had resolved to spend more time with us in the future. This affirmed for me that my dad, in his heart, wanted to heal his relationship with me. He, too, wanted us to be closer.

I feel as though I have my dad back as a supportive anchor in my life. I now look at his photograph on my bedside and talk to him daily. Looking back, in the first year after he passed, when I was just a teen, I often wondered if somehow he might return to us. I later judged this notion as naïve, as childlike wishful thinking that death was not really final. Now I see it differently. I believe that my soul always knew that my dad was with me in spirit, even though his physical form was gone. My wise self has always been in tune with his presence. He *would* return, as soon as I chose to reach out to him in my heart.

Each of us can call on deceased loved ones and ancestors for love, guidance, and even practical assistance if we consciously nurture our relationships with them. It's a matter of intention—of calling the person's presence into our hearts. If we intend to keep our connections, strengthen them, or create them anew, we absolutely have the spiritual power to do so. The power of love knows no physical bounds.

 Exercise: *Relationship Magic*

The following meditation-visualization practice is a powerful practice for connecting with loved ones and healing relationships. Is there a relationship from your past or present that you would like to nurture, strengthen, mend, or heal?

Bring this person to mind now.

Close your eyes, take in some nice deep breaths, and continue breathing until you feel your body relax. Call on your soul to fully embody your presence. Imagine, sense, and feel that you are connecting with your soul, your heart.

Feel the unconditional love your wise and loving spirit has for you. Feel it all the way through, like a pink healing light coming down from the heavens, through the crown of your head, traveling down to the tips of your toes and moving back up to your crown again. Allow this healing light to relax you even more.

Now travel in your imagination to a beautiful and peaceful place in nature—someplace you've been before or a place that your Spirit guides you. Visualize yourself and the other person together in this serene location of your own creation. See yourself in your mind's eye sitting across from the partner with whom you would like to feel more lovingly connected. It doesn't matter if you do not see them visually. Simply sense their presence. Visualize, imagine, sense, and feel a white healing light filling up the entire space. Imagine that the person has a soul flame in their heart. See the flame getting bigger and bigger until it fills their entire body.

Visualize and imagine, sense or feel that your heart is a gemstone, like an emerald, ruby, or rose quartz. See the same for your partner. Imagine that you are sending love and light from the jewel in your heart to the jewel in their heart. See and feel the love and light flowing back and forth between you.

In this safe space you have created in your imagination, the two of you are now able to relate on a soul level. Regardless of external events causing a disconnect or hurt between you, the soul is able to sense, feel, and transmit unconditional love. Feel the healing light embrace both of your souls. Allow the light and love to bring a sense of peace and serenity to your being.

We are exchanging telepathic messages of love or fear with others all the time, even when we're not aware of it. Being in this relaxed, loving place allows you to communicate with your partner so that they can receive your message in a nonthreatening way. Go ahead and speak from your heart. Let your partner know that your relationship is important—that they matter to you. Let them know that you desire a resolution with them.

Doing this exercise will shift the energy between the two of you. It's common to receive a phone call or email communication after doing this exercise. Or you may find yourself ready to make contact yourself, from a new place of compassion and understanding for your partner.

Your Soul Is Your Greatest Champion

I see now that my soul's inner nudge to take a Mexican adventure was divine direction in action. My life partner hadn't show up yet. I needed love and nourishment on many levels, so Spirit responded by sending me to Puerto Vallarta.

Once again, the answer to my prayers to receive support from my dad confirmed the power of staying connected to my inner guidance. I, of course, had no idea that Spirit was sending me to Vallarta for healing and life-affirming reasons beyond what I could even imagine.

As I said earlier, our inspired direction has far more wisdom—and much broader vision—than the ego mind's limited sight. Only the Divine has exclusive access to our life plan. Only the soul can see the big picture of our unfolding. Thank goodness the soul is keenly aware of the whole of our physical, emotional, mental, and spiritual needs, and how to meet them, when we are not.

I have found that this true caretaker of our spirit will nudge us to nourish any part of ourself that is out of balance. When I consciously let go enough to put my higher self in charge and follow it's direction, life gets easier, more fun, and sometimes even magical.

Your soul not only has a 360-degree view of your life, it is your biggest fan, greatest cheerleader, and most vocal champion. Partnering with your soul leads you to all the nurturing you need, including your soul family. Your soul will inspire you to follow your passion in part so you can meet soul family members. It will send you to places where you are more likely to connect with like-minded people whose presence lights you up and awakens you, even more, to your brilliance. Great things come with saying yes, even though we often cannot see what they are at the outset.

We Need Soul Family Like We Need Oxygen

My trip to Puerto Vallarta felt wonderfully magical, like heaven coming to bless me on earth! My new friendship with Miguel also opened my heart. For my birthday, he came to my angelic abode loaded with all the fixings for a wonderful celebration: his guitar, paints and a canvas, and delicious ingredients for an authentic Mexican meal that he would prepare for us. Dessert was an assortment of artfully made Mexican truffles from the local gourmet chocolate shop.

It seemed like delightful synchronicity that Miguel and I loved so many of the same songs from the seventies. We schmoozed about our all-time favorite movies and discovered that we both loved the same obscure film, *Harold and Maude*, a dark comedy with the theme of "being free," set to a Cat Stevens soundtrack. Because our connection felt so strong so immediately, I felt as though I had known Miguel for lifetimes. Rather than just beginning to know each other, it seemed like we were having a joyous reunion. We both felt like we were reminiscing rather than getting acquainted. Singing with him as he strummed his guitar made me incredibly happy—a feeling I can't even put words to. I just knew from the start that there was something very special about our connection. I could tell we were close friends from the same soul family.

Another thing that made this clear to me was how Miguel related to me. "I told my oldest daughter," he confided in a genuine tone that made me feel he was sincere, "that I have met an angel. You are a blessing to Vallarta with your light," he said from his heart. "You are inspiring a lot of people just with your presence." His words did not feel like a romantic gesture. Rather, Miguel was seeing me, witnessing my true essence, on a soul level. In other words, he was commenting on how he perceived me as a spiritual being, rather than on an ego or personality level. That he was seeing me in this way made me recognize instantly that we were soul friends.

Soul friends are able, when their hearts are open, to speak to one another from a place of unconditional love. It doesn't mean they don't have conflict or feel negative human emotions with one another. In fact, a soul friend may come into your life to facilitate a healing by behaving in ways that trigger painful emotions. But there is a special quality to a soul friend. When you are both coming from love, your connection feels out-of-this-world amazing! You may even feel that you understand each other without the use of words, as though you are connecting telepathically through your thoughts and feelings.

Your soul family is your "tribe." Finding your tribe makes you feel more supported, more anchored, and more connected to your life purpose. With this crucial support, you not only feel seen and heard for who you really are, but you feel more encouraged and uplifted to follow your heart and do what you came here to do on a spiritual level.

You may have grown up feeling different from, or not fully accepted by, one or more members of your biological family. If so, connecting with a soul family member for the first time can feel so profound that it catalyzes a spiritual awakening for one or both of you. At the very least, soul friend connections bring great comfort to your spirit. You feel fully seen, loved, and even celebrated by your soul friends.

You may fall more deeply in love with a soul friend than you have with anyone else because soul family members have the ability to reach you in ways that others do not. When you are with a soul friend and your two hearts are in sync, they are reflecting back your own radiant, pure love essence. This is the love Steve Winwood sings about in his song "Higher Love." It truly feels divine. Soul to soul love feels like the sun coming out in your heart.

The love exchanged between soul friends is a beautiful thing—it gives us a brand new lease on life. Soul friends give us the wind beneath our wings that lifts us into the realization of our dreams.

Soul Friends as Catalysts for Growth

Perhaps because we feel such immense love and connection with our soul friends, they can also serve as our greatest catalysts for growth. For example, after my first trip to Puerto Vallarta, I felt so embraced by my reunion with Ray and Brian, my deeper connection to my dad, and meeting Miguel and other soul family members who welcomed me with open arms, that I decided to return six weeks later. Miguel and I had stayed in touch by phone. He picked me up at the airport and even arranged for me to stay in a wonderful ocean-view condo, offered by one of his friends, free of charge. I was elated and couldn't wait to explore more of the area on adventurous day trips with him as my knowledgeable guide. I felt the same, openhearted connectedness that we had shared on my first trip.

But after a few days back in Vallarta, Miguel became less present. He had many reasons, but when he didn't show up one day at all as planned, I felt disappointed and hurt. We talked about what worked and did not work for each of us in relationship with one another. Despite being clear about my expectations, I began to see that

Miguel's way of being in relationship with me was causing more sadness and frustration than joy.

When someone we love cannot be present with us in the way we desire to be present with him or her, they are giving us an opportunity to expand our ability to love. I believe that we are being asked to surrender our ego's desire for them or the relationship to be something else, and accept them fully as they are.

This does not mean that we should disrespect our own needs in the process. Not at all. In fact, with Miguel, I received another opportunity to learn a lesson in self-love and discernment. It was clear to me that what he had to offer in a relationship with me was far less than my heart desired to give him. In the past, I had continued to show up in partnership with men who didn't have the ability or desire to create the level of intimacy I wanted. With Miguel, I recognized this early on and released all expectations before I invested my heart too deeply.

This did not change Miguel's love for me or mine for him on a soul level. I still feel his sincere desire for me to grow, prosper, and enjoy a beautiful life. Similarly, he had shared with me his plans to evolve his musical performances, and I, too, have a heartfelt enthusiasm for his success. I know that if I saw him today, our mutual soul love would still feel like the sun beaming brightly in our hearts, filling any room we found ourselves in with radiant light.

Soul family members may be with us for life. Or they may enter our lives for a specific reason: to show or teach us something we need to progress on our path. I see now that Miguel came into my life, and me into his, to expand our individual visions of the joy that we are each capable of experiencing with a life partner. He also taught me, through his actions, to take even more exquisite care of myself.

Soul friends can be like angels showing up and moving on when their mission is fulfilled. The reason may be as simple and profound as the potential to open your heart to even greater experiences of love.

You Are Never Alone

I was a high school junior, riding my bicycle home from school one sunny southern California afternoon as I always did. As I pulled into our driveway, I immediately sensed that something was "off." An uneasy feeling in my gut told me that this day is not life as usual. All the curtains were closed, not something my mom would ever do in the daytime—she loves the sunlight! I walked down the dark hallway toward her bedroom and found her standing in the threshold, tears streaming down her face. "Your father died today," she managed, sobbing. My heart was instantly broken.

Everything then seemed to move in slow motion. I don't remember having any thoughts in that moment. It felt like life as I knew it was ending suddenly and violently. And then, a bursting into an explosion of tears. My world had been completely shattered and the pieces were scattered everywhere. In my sixteen-year-old mind, I no longer had a father, and our family was now vulnerable in a very physical way as well.

My father had been the financial rock of our family. My mom had foregone a career to stay home with her four daughters. Now she was thrown into an emergency situation of needing to earn a good income after eighteen years of being a full-time homemaker and mother. I don't remember my mom reaching out to others for financial help or emotional support, although I'm sure she must have shared her sorrow with friends. Mostly, though, I had the sense that she, and we, were on our own to "survive" this crisis.

I woke up the next morning with flu-like symptoms that went on for weeks. I didn't see any point in going to school—my father was gone and along with him went my motivation. I see now that I was experiencing deep grief, but I had no words for it at the time. Fortunately, two weeks after his death, a team of angels showed up unannounced at our front door at 10 a.m. on a school day.

I opened the door to a huge surprise: my dance teacher, Mrs. Crockett, and twelve girls in our creative dance program, all beaming smiles my way. Together our dance production team created an annual spring show of student-choreographed dances. It was a big deal. Back then I would have said in my teenage enthusiasm, "Dance is my life!" We were all so passionate about it that we spent almost every lunch period and after-school time rehearsing for the big night.

Curtains still drawn, Mrs. Crockett and friends sat in a circle in my dark living room. "You have to come back to school … we're behind in rehearsals and we're ordering costumes … we need you!" One by one they gently yet firmly told me that my time at home was up.

Their palpable love was working on me, but still I wasn't convinced. "I don't know," I said. "I still feel really weak, and look at my hair, I haven't brushed it in two weeks!" A huge poof of tangles and knots sat on my head, making me look like Phyllis Diller with her teased hairdo.

In the most loving way, each girl began taking turns teasing the knots out of my long, extra-fine hair. They joked and laughed as we indulged in the old-fashioned donuts and apple juice they'd brought to lure me back to school.

This story still brings tears to my eyes. It was an extraordinary act of kindness and caring for my teacher to leave class and bring the whole dance troupe to my home in the middle of the school day to lift me out of my isolation. They did more than get me back to school … their love brought me back to life.

When you're in the middle of a transition, grieving loss is always part of the process. You are grieving the death of a dream—the way you *thought* life would be. You cannot navigate this shift without loving support. Knowing that others have your back, and allowing their help in practical ways, is immensely vital to coming through the passageway of change and emerging whole again.

Often those closest to you, such as your immediate family or even close friends, people who have been there for you in the past, are not able to be present. As in my case, they may be grieving as well, or they may be too close to the situation to give the unbiased, unconditional love and guidance you need. This is why, in the midst of transition, it is so important to connect with soul family and get the support you need.

Soul Mentors as Angels on Our Path

All of us have teachers or friends who have made deep and lasting impressions, even if their time with us has been relatively brief or only momentary. When someone affirms or awakens a belief in you, they may have come into your life not just for a reason, but "for a season." The higher purpose of your soul connection may be to alert you to a gift, talent, or ability you cannot yet see.

My freshman English teacher at UC Santa Barbara did this for me. I wish I could remember his name, but I certainly remember his sincere heart and words.

On a college placement English exam, I poorly identified the parts of speech and was placed in Subject A English, the basic class for students who, according to test results, needed help formulating sentences. I remember being surprised when I heard this since I had always gotten As in my high school English classes. Still, I went along with the university's placement decision and didn't give it much thought.

Then one day, my Subject A English professor copied my essay and distributed it to the class as an example of a well-written paper. I remember feeling flushed with delighted surprise as he began reading my paper and I recognized the words as mine! As he continued to read my work, excitement filled me and the feeling expanded into joy when he asked the class what they saw in my writing. Hearing the teacher and others sing praises of my work filled me with a new confidence. The next week, I turned in another essay, and again, the teacher chose it as the "model" essay. When it happened yet a third time, I was blown away by his appreciation of my writing. Later he took my essays to the English department committee, requesting that I be waived through English I. "Good news!" he told me one day. "You've been granted a waiver. You don't need to take freshman English. Choose Greek Mythology or any upper level class you want."

A year or two later, I ran into my professor while out wandering the streets of Santa Barbara one Saturday afternoon. We chatted briefly and before we said good-bye, he made a point of saying, "You are a talented writer. Never doubt your gift." Again, I got the chills, a sign that I had just received a message of higher guidance. He was being my angel along the path, acting as a divine spokesperson and cheerleader for my unfolding destiny.

Years later, when I found myself magnetically drawn to spiritual growth books and authors, I wondered if I could someday possibly write my own book. My English professor's words came back to me. I flashed back to sitting in class, seeing my paper on every student's desk and feeling the thrill of recognizing the words as my own. My memory took me back to meeting him on the street. I heard his affirming words resonate in my heart and mind. *Never doubt your writing gift.* His confidence in my writing ability is largely responsible for me believing I could write a book that would make a positive difference for others.

Soul mentors, like my English professor, show up to awaken you to the gifts and talents that you came here to share in this lifetime. Barbara Sher, career coach and best-selling author, says, "What you love is what you're gifted at."[10] Even if you haven't fully developed a specific talent yet, don't discount it as a natural gift. If you are feeling called to write, dance, sing, play an instrument, or be a better communicator, scientist, or lover, trust your calling. Sometimes it only takes one person, maybe even a quiet voice in a sea of dissenters, to remind you of something you came here to express or contribute.

 Exercise: *Resurrecting Your Gift*

Is there something in your life that you would secretly love to do? A hobby, interest, or even potential passion that you are not exploring because you're convinced it won't "get you anywhere?"

Is there a dream you've given up on because someone in authority, a parent or teacher perhaps, said you didn't have the talent to succeed?

- Take a moment to get quiet and reflect in silence. Scan your life from birth to the present. Was there a moment when someone or something—an experience of recognition or simply your own joy—gave you the inner *yes* to explore this talent?

- Conversely, was there a time when a critic negated one of your talents?

- What effect did this have on your inspiration and passion?

- How might you resurrect this gift or passion that was either celebrated or diminished?

Recognizing Your Soul Family

Soul family members, on the deepest level, have your best interests at heart. They genuinely want you to succeed. They applaud your achievements and champion your cherished heart's desires. With soul family, you feel as though you can be your true self, quirks and all. You feel comfortable showing them your vulnerable edges. You feel safe confiding your fears and worries. You know you can turn to them when you need encouragement. Your soul friends are your most adamant cheerleaders. They truly want to see you soar and fulfill your life purpose. They genuinely embrace and cheer on your fulfillment in the deepest sense.

Who is in your soul family? Soul family members come in all forms and may play different roles in your life. They may be a teacher, spiritual guide, friend, sibling, child, lover, spouse or ex-spouse, colleague, or mentor. To experience the loving support, guidance, and recognition from soul friends, you need to first become aware of who they are.

For example, at the age of thirteen, Carol had decided she no longer wanted to be my best friend. My family had relocated from our California home to Arizona in the middle of my eighth grade school year. All of us were miserable there. When my dad got a transfer back to California, I called Carol to express my elation that we were moving back home. That's when she broke the news. She was done with me. She recounted all the things "wrong" with me—all the reasons she'd made the decision to dump me, and I was devastated. I returned to school that fall without a best friend.

The first day back to class, I met Shelley in the girls' bathroom. She took one look at my sad face, asked what was wrong, and when I told her the story, she didn't miss a beat. She put her arm around me and announced with enthusiasm, "Well you just need to come be part of our group!" We had an instant connection: the mark of a true soul friend.

We have been a supportive presence in each other's lives ever since that moment. In retrospect, I can see that my own soul orchestrated this gift cloaked in loss and sadness. I was ready for a more heart-centered, soul-connected friendship—I was ready for what counselor Jan Santora calls "great love." I would not have sought this out had the Universe not first cleared the space by closing the door on my "best friend" status with Carol.

If you are in touch with your soul, actively growing and living your purpose, you may find that relationships shift along with you. Friendships may come and go or shift into a different rhythm. Maybe you lose touch with someone with whom you used to spend a lot of time. Especially in times of transition, certain people may leave your life for a time or seemingly for the foreseeable future. As you expand into a more authentic expression of your true self, it is normal to see this change in your relationships. As you grow, the way you relate to others and find others relating to you often changes as well.

Allow yourself to feel the feelings that arise and grieve any sense of loss. Know that the Law of Attraction is always at work. A void creates an opening to be filled. New friends are always on their way, especially when we consciously put out the intention to attract them. Often, though, a lag time between an ending and a new beginning brings a period of loneliness and isolation. In these times, especially, it is vital to get support. If you feel alone, partnering with a mentor, coach, or counselor makes a huge difference. We all need caring, loving people who believe in us wholeheartedly—people who can see and cherish the beauty and truth of who we are when we cannot see it ourselves.

Finding Your Tribe

Following your soul's calling always involves some sort of letting go. It may simply be the release of a way of seeing life and opening to a new, more expansive vision of what's possible. Growing and evolving does not require walking away from anything that you cherish. It's important to remember that you always have a choice and you don't have to leave anything you don't want to.

Occasionally, however, saying yes to your heart entails the emotional decision of leaving a relationship, marriage, church group, community, or job. Sometimes you walk away from more than one of these anchoring structures. Whenever a primary life structure dissolves, you experience the loss at the most primal level. You lose your tribe. You lose the tribal sense of belonging that you need to feel safe and secure in the world. This is true even if you don't feel fully loved and accepted by your family of origin, spouse, significant other, or co-workers. In fact, the fear of losing this security can keep you wedded to situations—whether personal or work—in which your heart and soul are crying out to be freed. It takes tremendous, and sometimes unfathomable, courage to say yes to your soul's urging to move on.

Even if you have received powerful messages from your guidance to let go, your sense of rootedness is nevertheless temporarily dislodged. It helps to remember that this is only temporary. The soul would not guide you to let go if it was not also ushering you into new territory where you can plant your roots even deeper than before. With your soul's unwavering love and support and the intention to feel safe and secure, you are fully supported in finding your new tribe.

For example, when I had experienced one too many long evenings googling "how to recover from divorce," I realized I was searching in the wrong place. What my spirit really wanted was to be in communion with others who were going through the same thing. I was a teacher of self-discovery and spiritual transformation—I had plenty of tools to heal and reinvent my life! I was also receiving support from a spiritual counselor and coach. Despite these wonderful resources, I also needed to connect with my tribe: others who were going through the exact same transition I was.

There is no better comfort for the soul than spending time with people who are experiencing similar emotions, life upheaval, and grief. In witnessing one another's stories, you know you are not alone. You are given a safe container in which to feel your emotions so they can heal.

My soul nudged me to create a workshop series called *Reinventing Your Life After Divorce*. I knew there was a community need for this, and my participants confirmed my knowing a thousand times over. I offered a number of these series over the course of two years. Feedback such as *you saved my life* and *without this group I would have drowned in my own tears* was common. What they were saying was: *You gave me a new place to belong. You showed me that I wasn't alone. You helped me find me, at a time when who I thought I was had disappeared.*

What I remember most is the tremendous sense of gratitude that participants felt as a result of finding a new tribe. One grateful participant, Suzanne, hosted a loving dinner, inviting me and all the participants of every *Reinventing Your Life* group that I had facilitated to her home to honor the life-changing transformation she received from the experience.

Her class group later invited me to join one of their reunion meetings. They let me know that they had all been meeting regularly, socializing and having fun. Their enthusiasm and love for one another was palpable. They joked about how downtrodden they looked and felt when they entered the workshop, and the transformation that brought them back to life in the process.

Sometimes you think you'll never emerge from the darkness. And then one day the sun comes out in your heart, and you remember who you really are. You feel the stirrings of wholeness, of vigor, maybe even celebration. A brand new self—stronger, more vibrant, more beautiful than before—is coming alive. If you let them, tears of happiness and thanksgiving will flow.

Never doubt that you *will* emerge as the butterfly again.

 Exercise: *Connect with Your Soul Family*

Take a moment to get quiet and reflect. Name the people in your life whom you consider to be your soul family:

Have you expressed your love to these people lately? You may want to write a note of appreciation to one or more of them. Appreciation brings more soul family love into your life. The more you appreciate and give thanks for what you desire, the more its presence expands in your world.

Here's another way to intentionally call in your soul family: what qualities would you like to experience in your soul family members? Take a few moments to reflect on these qualities. Write down how you desire to feel with your soul family, such as, "With my soul friends, I feel appreciated, seen and unconditionally loved."

- With my soul family, I desire to feel …

- The quality I would most appreciate in a soul friend is …

One way to call soul friends into your life is to begin to *be* what you want to receive. Are there any places in your life where you could be more of this yourself? I invite you to practice with people who are in your life now. Consciously appreciate them, see their true essence, and endeavor to give them your unconditional love.

The following meditation will powerfully put your intention in motion. You may want to read the words into a recorder first so you can do the meditation with your eyes closed. Or take turns with a loved one, guiding each other into this deep relaxation to connect with your soul family.

 ## Meditation: *Calling in Your Soul Family*

Begin to take in a few nice deep breaths. Breathe in, and as you exhale, let go. Know that you are in the perfect place to receive guidance. It does not have to take long to receive an insight, a revelation, or to connect with your soul family. I am guiding you with the intention of connecting you with your own soul and those kindred souls who are ready to come into your life.

Feel yourself now becoming more and more relaxed. With every breath, you are letting go. Allow your shoulders to drop down and relax. Soften the muscles in your face and around your eyes. Soften the back of your neck. Feel your connection to the earth. The earth is supporting you. Spirit is supporting you.

Now call in your connection to your higher power. With your breath you can consciously connect to Spirit. Visualize and imagine rays of beautiful violet light shining down from the heavens onto the crown of your head. See, sense, and feel these rays of light going straight through your crown—your seat of inspiration and connection to Spirit. This light is moving from your crown through your body until it touches into the thriving center of the earth. Breathe in this violet light. With your breath, you are connecting to mother earth.

I invite you now to go with me into a beautiful, peaceful place in nature. See, feel, and sense yourself walking along a gorgeous tree-lined path. Notice the brilliant fall colors—golds, oranges, and reds. Feel the sun shining on your body. Every cell of your body now opens to receive this healing sunlight. The sunlight is a reflection of you, your radiance, your brilliance. If you could see yourself the way those in Spirit see you, you would know what a magnificent being you are.

And as you walk along this tree-lined path, you see a beautiful gate, covered in flowers. You step in through this gate and walk into a sacred place of your own creation. This may be a sacred, secret garden or simply a sanctuary in nature. This place resonates to the vibration of your own soul. This place—the trees, the flowers, the earth—knows you intimately; it knows your soul, it knows your path. And so you feel a warm, kindred connection, a sense of peace, a sense of joy, and sense of knowing what you are here for.

In this beautiful sacred place there is a circle, a sacred circle, like a sanctuary. Find this sanctuary now and allow yourself to go there. Stand in the center of this sacred circle. Imagine, sense, and feel that you are surrounded by your soul family. Become aware that there are beings in your circle who are here just for you. Your circle may include people who are in your life right now, as well as new friends you will meet in the near future. Even perhaps ancestors who have passed on who have shown up to support you now. You may also sense spirit guides or angels or all of the above.

Look around your circle and notice who is here for you. Take a breath and begin to receive their love. Open your palms to receive the comfort and support of your soul family. Open your heart to let in this love. Beams of light are shining on you from all of these beings who love and cherish you. Take this love and light in through your palms, through your heart, through your eyes. Feel it enter every cell in your body. Allow yourself to receive it fully.

Take a moment now to send gratitude to every being in your circle.

Travel now to another place in your sanctuary, maybe next to a tree, where you can invite and call into your life the presence of a future soul friend or soul mate. Call in this new soul family member by simply feeling this intention in your heart.

Imagine that you are about to see or sense the presence of a new member of your soul family coming to meet you. On the count of six, this presence will be felt. One … two … three … four … now, look around the tree … and five … six … coming into view now … see, sense, or feel your new soul friend or mate. Whatever comes is perfect. Know that even if nothing comes, you are planting powerful seeds of intention beneath the surface of your conscious awareness—powerful seeds that will come to fruition in the days, weeks, and months to come.

Begin to walk back now through the gate that you entered, returning on a path that is leading you back to the present moment. Come back to an awareness of your body. Slowly move and wake up your toes, feet, fingers, and hands. And when you are ready, gently open your eyes.

7

# Unwavering Self-Love

You yourself, as much as anybody in the entire Universe, deserve your love and attention.

~ Buddha

Self-deprivation is soul deprivation. It comes at a hefty price. When I'm deciding between self-care or sacrificing my own well-being, I imagine transitioning at my death. Will I look back and wish I had taken more risks and opened myself to more adventures? Will I say, "Good thing I was super careful with money?" Or will it be more like, "Gosh, you know, I was actually more free than I gave myself credit for. I wish I would have said yes to my heart more often. Look at the potential for joy that I wasted."

~ A Journal Entry

I remember one evening when I was nine years old, my parents coming home from a dinner out. We were newly living in a suburb of Atlanta, Georgia. My dad had been transferred across the country for work, and my sisters and mom and I were doing our best to acclimate after leaving our family home in southern California. On this particular night, I was in my bedroom, almost asleep, when I heard my mom and dad walk into the house, yelling at one another. My father exclaimed to my mother, "Fine, if you want a divorce, go ahead and get one!"

To my nine-year-old-self their dialogue was shattering. My parents—getting divorced? This was the first time I had heard of this. It was even more jarring to hear the news delivered by desperate-sounding adults in the dark hallway of a house that didn't yet feel like mine. I had witnessed many more arguments between them in the years prior to this. My parents' fights were so upsetting to my sensitive nature that there were moments I would sit quietly in my bedroom, praying that they *would* divorce, so we wouldn't have to listen to them raise their voices in anger anymore. Months after that argument in Georgia, we all moved back to California and my mom and dad stuck it out for five more years until they finally make a decision to end their marriage.

My parents didn't know how to discuss their differences and reach compromises in peaceful, respectful ways. As a result, they also did not know how to teach my sisters and me how to resolve conflict. Although we had many wonderful moments of fun and loving play in my house, there was also plenty of dissension and fighting.

If you had asked me as a child whether I felt loved, I would have said, "Yes! My mom greets me every morning with a hug and a kiss." I did feel very much loved by my mom and often by my dad as well. However, years later, I realized that because of the chaos in our home environment, I often did not feel safe and secure.

Few of us received unconditionally loving parenting. In my coaching practice, I have worked with many clients who also did not feel completely safe growing up. Some were emotionally or physically abused by adults they trusted. Since most of our caregivers did not receive unconditionally loving parenting themselves, they could not give us what they never received or learned to give.

Some of my clients have talked about their "wounding" experiences for years in therapy, yet they still found themselves stuck and unfulfilled in their careers or relationships. They come to me with a strong desire to graduate from an identity of "I am wounded," "unloved," "undeserving," or "not enough." They are tired of feeling limited by the love they didn't get from their parents and weary of feeling victimized by past circumstances that, as children, they had no power to change. They are ready to finally free themselves to say yes to their hearts' desires.

When a primary structure in your life—a relationship or job, or both—is threatened or ends, past childhood emotions of feeling unsafe or insecure are often triggered. Losing your connection to your tribe of family or co-workers compromises your sense of belonging.

One thing is true: we all need to feel safely anchored to even contemplate living our dreams.

To muster the courage to release what has run its course and step further into your potential, you need to feel that you are deeply loved and cherished. How do you do this?

First, I want to acknowledge that having your experiences of loss and pain witnessed is an essential part of healing. At a certain point, however, retelling the story of wounding or traumatic experiences only reinforces that you are the victim, rather than the powerful creator, of your life. Deep and lasting healing on a level that frees and transforms must engage your innate creativity to change your perceptions. Whether or not you are aware of it, your soul is guiding you to create a new, more empowering story—a story that you are nourished and loved and poised to take off on a joyful adventure of new possibility.

The following self-love practices invoke the power of your imagination to create a new vision. By reaching inside and loving your inner little child, you are effectively starting fresh, creating an experience of safety and unconditional acceptance. By witnessing the truth of your inner child as pure love, as fully capable of realizing your dreams, you are celebrating your true gifts and talents. These practices of inner nourishment provide you with a solid foundation upon which to begin happily scrawling the details of your next life chapter.

Self-love is the most powerful healing balm you can administer. With my clients, I've witnessed breakthrough after breakthrough from the consistent practice of two simple self-love practices. I am confident that, in applying these tools, you can experience the same life-changing results. You only need to be willing to take a new adventure into the land of self-love and appreciation.

This is the most important journey you will ever take, and it only requires one thing: your willingness to give yourself the love that the child within you needs to feel safe and to thrive. Are you ready?

Self-Love: The Most Powerful Healing Balm

I call this a magical practice, because after years of using it with myself and offering it to clients, its profound healing results continue to amaze me. Clients come back to my office feeling changed: more vital, refreshed, and alive. It's as if they are becoming new again, and they are. This is the power of self-love.

To go out of your comfort zone and go after your dreams with gusto, you need to feel anchored and tethered to something you can trust. Cultivating a partnership with your soul is one route to feeling this core stability. Another is being loved by a truly nurturing parent who you know, in every cell of your body, has your back. A nurturing parent is someone you can turn to for emotional support when life throws you a curveball.

The wonderful truth is, you have the power to create this nourishing and unconditionally loving force of goodness within yourself.

Being your own nurturing parent is vital, because whenever you're inspired to break out and entertain a new possibility for your life, the ego balks and the inner critics get loud. You need an inner cheerleader to say, *"No matter what those voices are saying, they are not speaking the truth. The truth is, you have all you need to make this happen. I believe in you. You are enough! You can do this!"*

The following self-love practice was inspired by the work of spiritual teachers Louise Hay and Darren Weissman. This practice has worked magic in my life. When practiced consistently, this exercise can bring you phenomenal healing results as well.

I suggest doing it every day for forty days. Throughout many ancient wisdom traditions, the Bible, and the Kabbalah, the Jewish mystical text, the number forty holds tremendous transformational significance. Jesus fasted in the desert for "forty days and forty nights" in order to awaken to his true mission. Noah's ark sailed for forty days and forty nights to preserve life. Like the Bible, the Kabbalah teaches that forty days is the necessary period of time to shift your consciousness into a new way of being. After forty consecutive days of delivering the same message of love to your inner child, the truth that you are safe and secure will be beautifully wired into your subconscious mind. You will feel more relaxed and more open to new possibilities in your life.

Exercise: *Be the Voice of Love*

Look in the mirror directly into your eyes. You connect with your soul through your eyes. Imagine that you are talking to your inner little boy or girl. Imagine the sweet, vulnerable child inside of you that needs to know he or she is safe and loved unconditionally, regardless of what's going on in life. Now speak to your inner child with sincere encouragement and love. Say: *I love you. I love you exactly the way you are.*

After you have this down, you might want to expand your message of love. Have fun with it. Tell your inner child what *you* would have wanted to hear as a child.

For example:

> *Good morning, beautiful (or handsome)! Look at you … could you possibly be more gorgeous?! Guess what, today we're going to have an amazing day! I love you so much, and I want nothing less for you. Do you know that you are the sun in my solar system, and that you deserve the best? No one could be more important to me than you. I will make sure all of your needs are met. Today we're going to make magic together! I love you more than words could ever say. Beloved, I adore you.*

It's common to tear up when you do this practice. You may be telling your inner child words that he or she has never heard before. I love it when I cry doing this exercise because it affirms that a healing was needed. Feeling is always healing.

Cultivating your inner nurturing voice is a process that may take some practice to get comfortable with. Do this for forty days straight and the positive results will astound you. It takes just one minute, twice a day, for a total of two minutes per day.

I suggest doing this in the morning and before bed when you brush your teeth, because most of us brush our teeth twice a day. It's easier to create a new habit when you associate it with an action you already do regularly without thinking. Beginning in the morning will also infuse your day with an uplifting self-loving intention. Intention is powerful because it sets the energy moving in the direction of your desired result. As I've said before, where intention goes, energy will flow.

Don't be discouraged if talking to your inner child in the mirror feels difficult at first. You may be distracted by lines around your eyes, or hear the inner critic point to so-called "flaws" in your facial features. This is not you—this is resistance talking. Say *thank you for sharing* and keep going.

Your purpose is to heal through loving yourself, which is a powerful intention and well worth moving through resistance for.

By the way, when I do my mirror exercise and notice my facial lines, I now affirm the beauty in those as well. That's a lot of progress for me! You are capable of the same.

Mark off each of the forty days of mirror practice on your calendar. You might even want to buy yourself a package of gold stars to celebrate each day's success.

Permission to Be You, Just as You Are

Your dreams are fueled by the passion of your spirit and the creative child within you. Take a breath, relax, and travel back in your memory to the last time you had an inspired idea or moment of joy. Go way back if necessary—back to a time when you felt vital and alive. Do you remember the feeling? If not, take a few more breaths and go into your imagination. Let yourself sense, visualize, or imagine you being happy. What are you doing? Consciously allow yourself to feel the excitement of a new possibility.

Engaging your inner child's imaginative spirit helps move you into a new expression. To feel free, your young creative muse needs to know that she is held in loving arms—that she can count on you to always be there for her. Your inner child needs to know that he is loved, exactly the way he is. If your inner child doubts this, they will opt out of your creative process. They will go on strike, bringing up any manner of resistance to your soul's unfolding.

Loving your inner child is therefore a necessary tool for coming alive and saying yes to your dreams.

As I mentioned above, whenever your soul attempts to wake you up to the next destination on your path, an ardent committee of inner critics gets activated. They line up like prison guards, zealously guarding the prison exit, keeping your soul-inspired, passionate self from freeing him- or herself and saying yes. These guards can see only one way, and, of course, it's "the right way."

The inner critics' right way means staying in the same exact place that brought on the pain, restlessness, or extreme discomfort to begin with. Inner critics invariably push you to remain inside the lines of your current life, even if you are miserable. They are stalwart protectors of the scared ego. They will do anything to keep you from breaking the rules that no longer fit the expanded being that you have become.

Which reminds me of my client Steve. He and his wife had lived "parallel lives" for years. He traveled extensively for work, and for long periods of time they even lived in different states. Practically speaking, they had been separated for more than a year, but never formally so. Steve saw his wife as his "best friend," but felt no passion, emotionally, mentally, or physically, which caused him great sadness and angst. He admitted that their marriage had died years earlier, but despite his sincere desire to kindle passion he had never truly felt, he couldn't bring himself to let it go.

The rules in his head said that "a good man" stays with his wife and best friend. He was also beating himself up for an affair that he had ended and revealed to his wife, along with a promise to try and make their marriage work. But he couldn't get it to work, and this made him feel woefully inadequate. Add in the affair, which he deeply regretted as an "unforgivable act" for which he felt he deserved to be punished.

In our weekly phone coaching sessions, I led Steve in a meditation-visualization to love and nourish his inner child. Each of these meetings brought him deep emotional release and healing. He began to get to know this child part of himself that had needs and desires. He listened to what they were, and kept giving his inner child more love, more playtime, and most important, the permission and freedom to be just who he was.

One day on our coaching call, Steve had something important to tell me. "I think I finally got it," he said.

I could hear the lightness of a breakthrough coming through his voice.

"I realize I've been keeping myself in prison. I've been trying to live by rules that aren't even mine. I've been waiting for someone to free me, but I'm the one holding the key! I realize that I'm not loving myself or my wife by staying in our marriage out of duty. She and I—both of us—deserve better."

Steve realized that his guiding genius was being drowned out by an inner committee of prison guards that didn't have his best interests at heart. These inner critics, the ones who continually berated his past actions and told him what a "good" man should do, did their very best to keep him locked up. They were the gatekeepers to his freedom, until he woke up to the truth that he—and love—held the key. Loving himself and his wife meant letting go.

Steve shared with me the effect the meditation-visualization practice had on freeing himself. When he first met his inner little boy in the healing visualization, little Steve was a bit aloof and indifferent to him. But as the adult Steve continued to show up, love, and reassure this child as a nurturing parent would, he began to open up and receive his love. After a number of repetitions, little Steve trusted that he was in fact, safe and loved. The courage Steve needed to follow his soul's direction followed.

This meditation-visualization has brought deep healing to clients and to me. It is a cornerstone of my work, because it brings life-changing results when repeated over time. If you desire a powerful, positive life transformation, I encourage you to do this practice, like the mirror exercise, once a day for forty days.

 Exercise: *Loving Your Inner Child Meditation-Visualization*

Go ahead and get comfortable sitting in your chair or lying down. Gently close your eyes. Relax and breathe. Scan your body now for any places that are ready to let go. Relax the small muscles around your eyes, let go in your jaw, soften the back of your neck, and drop your shoulders. That's good. This is your time. Time to give yourself a gift—time to connect to your inner wisdom.

There is nothing you have to do but let go and relax. I invite you to take in a few nice deep, cleansing breaths. On the inhale, breathe in peace. Take in life, energy, and abundance. On the exhale, breathe out everything else.

Release everything that came before this today. With each breath, allow yourself to let go, more and more. You may notice your mind chattering as you focus solely on your breath. That's okay. Just notice it. See the chatter passing like clouds. With every breath, allow yourself to relax even deeper. Go beneath the chatter now to a place of peace and calm … to the place you go at night just before you fall asleep. That's good.

Now allow your breath to drop you down to the next deeper … quieter layer. More and more, you find yourself very relaxed.

You are safe. This is your journey. At any time during this meditation, you are free to follow my words or journey in your own way. You are not alone, you are so supported and you are being guided.

Going even deeper now, deeper into the wise part of you that knows … knows that no matter what is going on in your life and around you, in the bigger picture of life, all is truly well.

I am about to take you now to a beautiful place in nature where you can relax even more. I want you to visualize and imagine, sense and feel that you are walking on a peaceful tree-lined path. Notice the colors … the air … perhaps there's a slight breeze … feel the warm sun on your body. Notice what you're wearing—allow it to be something you feel really good in. Feel the earth under your feet.

Up ahead you see a garden gate—the entrance to your own secret, sacred garden. Walk through the gate now. This is your very own garden to imagine and create as your heart desires. Take a few moments to visualize, sense, imagine and take in the beauty of your garden.

Breathe in the peace of this sacred place—the joy of being here where all is well. You are at ease. You feel a sense of hopefulness, like the promise of spring returning. You are coming back to life.

Looking around your garden now, you see a place where a child is playing. As you approach the child, you see that he or she is you, when you were a little girl or boy. The child turns to see you, lights up, and comes toward you. Greet your child and embrace him or her.

Look into his or her eyes and feel the love between you—a strong bond. You are one. This child is your freedom, your joy, your creative spark. This child loves you. You love one another unconditionally.

Spend a few moments with your inner child. Stroke her hair, hold her close, let her know you will always be here for her.

Now look into your inner child's eyes. Tell him: I love you so much. I believe in you! Nothing you could do would ever disappoint me. I love you just the way you are. Look into your inner child's eyes and tell him what you see in him. Tell him what you see that is special about him.

Let your child know that no matter what happens, you will always be here—that you will never abandon him: "I will never, ever leave you. You are the most important person in my life."

Embrace your child, saying goodbye just for now. Release her now to play in the garden.

Stand up now, walk back out through the gate, and back on the tree-lined path. See this scene fade as you come back into present time. Come back into your body, and begin to wake up your body, moving your fingers and toes, neck and shoulders, and stretching if you'd like. Come back to your breath, back to the present moment, and slowly become aware of your presence in the room. When you're ready, gently open your eyes.

Note: When you return, state your name and current age aloud. This will bring you consciously back into your adult self.

No Matter What Happens, You Are Enough

I believe that we are born knowing, deep down, that we came here to be the heroes of our own lives. On some level we know that the soul is urging us on to awaken to our true nature as "spiritual warriors." Spiritual warriors, in that we sense the fire of our destiny burning in our hearts. This fire is our desire to live out our passionate mission and express our true nature in ever expanding expressions. The spiritual warrior's path is a path of courage. We need courage because, from a very early age, we are told "no" so many times that we forget who we really are. We lose sight of our divine essence. We forget that as infinite beings sourced in unconditional love, we have the power to create our dreams.

Things happen that make us doubt our gifts and talents. We hit bumps in the road and make meaning about them—meaning that tells us we're not beautiful enough, talented enough, young enough, or smart enough to realize our dreams. We forget the truth—that no matter what happens in life—we *are* enough!

For example, a couple of months ago, I was driving into the garage of the grocery store where my youngest daughter, Molly, works. I'd been out of town for the Labor Day weekend and needed to fill my refrigerator. I also missed Molly and was really looking forward to seeing her. But as I pulled into my parking spot ... well, let me just say that it is never a good thing when your car makes direct contact with another vehicle! Yes, I felt that awful feeling you get when you hear a scraping sound and you know there's no going back—that the damage has already been done—and *you've* done it.

I have to say, I felt very blessed that the lady whose car I scraped was unusually kind and compassionate with me. It was my doing, but she practically apologized to me for the fact that it happened in the first place. Still, walking into the store, I was feeling upset as I thought about my $500 insurance deductible. Inside I could hear the voice of the inner critic, "You could have avoided this. If only you had been more grounded, this wouldn't have happened!"

I walked into the store and went straight to the sample table, hoping to see my daughter and receive a much-needed hug. She wasn't there, but another store clerk greeted me and asked me how I was. In that moment, I made a split-second decision to be vulnerable. "Actually," I responded, "I'm feeling pretty shaken up. I feel badly, both because I just scraped a car in your parking lot and did damage to someone else's car, and because I have a hefty deductible." Just naming and sharing my true feelings, I felt relieved. The clerk and another shopper began to give me their sympathy. A few moments later, my daughter walked up and gave me a big, long hug.

To my surprise, an hour later at home, I discovered a bouquet of gorgeous creamy, salmon-tipped roses in my entryway. Turns out my daughter's boyfriend, Anthony, heard what happened and anonymously left the flowers inside my door.

When I saw the roses, it hit me. Despite the difficult challenges that life brings, all that really matters is love. In fact, when life feels hard or disappointing, what we're missing is love. We are temporarily separated from love's essence: compassion, tenderness, and self-acceptance. The situation or circumstances have triggered an emotion that is distancing us from the truth of love. We are forgetting that we *are* love. Love is the most powerful healing balm.

We All Need a TLC Plan

In life, "stuff," like this car accident, happens. You can easily get triggered and react in ways that aren't self-loving or helpful. There is another way. You can pause and give yourself and any others involved compassion and tender loving care (TLC). Here's a self-loving TLC Plan to help you move through life's inevitable bumps.

1. Take a breath. Name and feel your emotion(s).

The emotion itself is not scary, although the ego believes it is. When you feel anxious, afraid, or worried, notice where you feel the emotion in your body. Put your hand on that place and name it. Say, I feel _____ _____.

You might also add this healing affirmation, Even though I feel _____ _____, I still totally and completely love and accept myself. This often brings instant relief.

2. Now connect with your heart. Ask, what do I need right now?

Allow yourself to fulfill your immediate needs. Be willing to take exquisite care of yourself.

3. Reach out for support.

Give yourself permission to be vulnerable with someone around whom you feel safe. You need your losses and emotions to be witnessed by loving others. Vulnerability is not a weakness—it's actually your strength. Being vulnerable gives you the chance to receive support.

4. Give yourself compassion.

Let go of judgment against yourself. If you judge others or yourself as right or wrong and place blame, you block your healing. Forgiveness isn't denying what happened or saying you would do it the same way again. We all learn from our mistakes. Forgiving yourself is letting go of your grievance.

5. Reframe the situation in love.

Where is this giving you an opportunity to love—yourself, others, or both? In truth, love is all that matters—we are all spirits of pure love.

6. Connect with your higher guidance.

Ask Spirit, your intuitive guidance, your spirit guides or angels, and/or your wise self to guide you.

I love the simple prayer: *Show me …*

For example, *Show me how to best take care of myself right now.*

Show me that you're here for me. Show me that I'm not alone.

Show me that even though it feels as if everything is falling apart right now, all is truly well.

A Game: *Daily Love in Action*

How many ways can you love yourself? I invite you to play a game.

Write the following love words down on a card and keep your card in your purse or wallet. Each day look at the card and choose one action word as a guiding intention for your day. Then imagine one tiny (or big) thing you can do to follow through.

Nurture	Admire	Respect
Nourish	Embrace	Celebrate
Cherish	Love	Comfort
Adore	Laugh	Sing Praises For
Delight In	Play	Encourage

- Add your own love words here …

- Today I choose to _____.

- The one tiny thing I will do is …

For example, today I choose to laugh.

The one tiny thing I will do to laugh is search *Funniest Home Videos* on YouTube and watch one that really cracks me up.

8

Nourishment Is Necessary

Dance, when you're broken open. Dance, if you've torn the bandage off. Dance in the middle of the fighting. Dance in your blood. Dance when you're perfectly free.

~Rumi

Being real and speaking your truth is all that matters. I read somewhere that next to food and water, all human beings really want is to be heard. Your soul needs this in order to thrive. Perhaps this is the magic recipe for reinventing your life—speaking up and letting your voice be heard.

~A Journal Entry

I once offered a wonderful workshop called *Nurturing Your Brilliance*. I put the word *nurturing* in the title because I've found that nourishing every aspect of your being—your body, mind and spirit—is absolutely vital to feeling good and keeping your energy high.

Your *brilliance* includes the sparkling gifts you came to offer the planet—your intelligence, creativity, beauty, love, wisdom, joy—your own unique expression of what lights you up. This is your meaningful contribution. Your brilliance is so specific to you that no one else could possibly deliver it in the same way. Your brilliance is your guiding genius. When you are in touch with your guiding genius, you feel uplifted and inspired to take the next step in your unfolding destiny.

As I've spoken about throughout this book, activating your brilliance lies in consciously nurturing a clear connection to your soul and universal support—the source of your inner wisdom. From this connection, you receive guidance about your next steps. You are also guided to what is calling for clearing or healing so you can move forward in joy. And often your soul simply nudges you to do something pleasurable and fun to increase your energy so you can be magnetic to that which your heart desires!

You sense, hear, and feel your higher guidance through the energetic connections of your body, mind, and spirit. I think of each of these as an energy system that needs your attention and tender loving care. They are like musical instruments that must be kept in tune in order to play beautiful melodies. Before playing a concert, musicians always tune their instruments first. They would laugh if you said, "You can do that later, just start playing your songs!" Yet that is what we tend to do with our physical, emotional, spiritual, and mental health. For example, you may feel exhausted—a sign that you need rest. Then the ego negates your need, saying, "You can rest later. You have a deadline; you don't have time to pause now." So you give in to the ego's pushing and resolve to power through anyway.

I've found that if I'm out of balance on any level—physically, mentally, emotionally, or spiritually—I have a harder time hearing the messages of my soul. Living a soul-inspired life makes nourishing your energy systems as necessary as breathing. If you truly want to free yourself to say yes to your heart, taking supreme care of yourself is non-negotiable.

Years ago, I thought of self-care as "a good thing to do" because investing in my well-being would increase my self-esteem. This is true, but then I discovered an even more compelling reason. I was working long hours when I began having a recurring dream:

> In my dream, I am walking along a path when a disturbing sight stops me in my tracks. Lying off to the side of the trail is an undressed baby who is so frail she needs IV fluids to survive. I wrap her in my coat and whisk her to the hospital.

Needless to say, my dream was sending me a message—it was a dramatic wake up call. At the time, I had convinced myself that hard work was what I needed to do. I wasn't aware that this overwork was me, operating in barely surviving mode. I was running on fear of not getting enough accomplished, rather than on the life-giving fuel of my soul's desire to thrive.

I realized that I wasn't trusting in the flow of life to support me. I made a decision to honor myself enough to set limits and healthy boundaries around work, no matter what my ambitious ego was pushing me to accomplish. I made a self-vow to slow down and move at a comfortable pace to build my career and care for myself in the process. After all, what is hard work worth if you are not nourished as you go? Working hard to get somewhere is a fear-based way of living, and it's impossible to live from fear and experience love and joy at the same time.

As soon as I made this inner commitment, I stopped having the recurring "barely-surviving" dream. I realized that no matter what was happening in my life, it was *the way* I was attending to things that determined how energized or depleted I felt. I resolved to put self-nurturing first, as an act of self-love. I knew that if I was going to fulfill my purpose—to be love in the world—I had to give myself the love I wanted to give and express to others and the planet.

✸ Exercise: *Make a Vow of Self-Care*

You are the foundation of your life. All success is sourced from the well of your well-being. Are you ready to commit to placing your self-care first? I invite you to put your commitment in writing. Writing it down makes it happen.

I, _____ , am hereby committing to a vow of self-care. I make a sacred promise to care for my body, mind, and spirit. I am open to receiving nudges from my soul/inner wisdom regarding any changes that I can make to increase my well-being and happiness. I am ready to take action to thrive! And so it is.

Signed in sincere love and commitment,

_____

Love Your Body

When I was a young teen, I was on a quest to improve myself. In our dance production class, I would silently compare myself to other dancers in my class. If I had her long legs, I thought, or her pretty nose, or her gorgeous long, thick hair, I would be so pretty.

I remember one day reading a feature article on being a teen model in *Seventeen Magazine*. Full-length, color photos of various models in the latest styles, along with their height and weight, graced the slick pages. I fixated on a model with an adorable bouncy-brunette hair cut and porcelain white skin. To me, she looked perfect. I took note of her height, which was 5' 7", the same as mine. She weighed 105 pounds, however, and my weight was 125. I was slender by most people's measurement, but setting my sights on looking just like this model, I would need to lose twenty pounds. I tried every starvation diet I could find to get down to this supposed ideal weight. But even at my lowest weight, I couldn't win. I was desperately discontent with the body I saw in the mirror.

I see now that it was my ego that was striving to improve how I looked, and the ego is never satisfied. It's a losing game because we can never be good enough, thin enough, beautiful enough, or perfect enough to please the ego.

In my not-yet spiritually mature mind, I thought the purpose of life was to improve and excel in all ways, including how I looked. I didn't realize the higher truth that now brings me deep peace and joy—none of us needs improving! We are not here to get ahead or achieve anything. It's the ego that sees something missing or wrong with us and immediately wants to fix it. The truth is, we are actually here for an entirely different—a much more exciting—reason. As spiritual beings having a human experience, our real purpose is to love and honor ourselves as we are—including our bodies.

I remember waking up to this truth when I heard a wise person say, "You have been given the exact body you need to fulfill your life's purpose." Everything about you has been perfectly designed to support you in living your life's design with aplomb. Ever since that day, I changed my quest from *improving* my body to *appreciating* the body I've been given.

This is a big stretch for many of us who have grown up sizing up our features and comparing ourselves to celebrities and fashion magazine idols. I suggest beginning with choosing to love one aspect of your physical self. One of my friends delights in her strong legs. Another loves her sexy curves. If you can't find anything you love about your body, begin by celebrating that your legs work—that you have the ability to take walks in nature, for example.

It can take some time and practice for the new way of feeling about your body to register in your cells and then your behavior, but if you stay with it, your self-appreciation will bring wonderful results.

When you accept and appreciate your body, it can naturally take the shape it is meant to have for you to feel healthy and vital. Like anything, when you love and care for your body, it responds by feeling better. In this space of self-love, any "extra pounds" fall away more easily. You'll be motivated to exercise because when you love your body, you'll want to take care of it. Taking care of your body will not only make you feel more energized and alive, it will give you a huge boost in joyful living.

Listening to the Messages of Your Body

I've also found that the more in tune I am with what my body needs to flourish, the more it tells me what it needs. My intention to nourish my body opens the flow to guidance. As soon as I committed to a thriving body, I began to get nudges from my soul.

For example, I started receiving recurring inner guidance on small changes I could make in my diet. Eat more veggies, especially greens, was one. Another was, cut down on sugar. I didn't want to hear that one. I love bread and pastries! But I noticed that when I reduced my carb and sugar intake, my energy increased, and I didn't have the energy crashes. My higher guidance also nudged me to drink more water. The body needs one quart for every fifty pounds of body weight, which for most of us is considerably more than the standard eight glasses we were taught was enough. I now bring a one-quart water bottle with me everywhere I go. Staying hydrated makes a huge difference in how I feel.

Every symptom of pain, illness, fatigue, lethargy, or low energy is your body talking to you, letting you know that it needs attention. Listening to your body's messages honors your connection with its wisdom and yields wonderful, life-giving results. Your specific physical needs are as unique as you are. What nourishes me—what my body loves—may be different from what helps your body thrive. Your inner guidance, and the upcoming exercise, will let you know.

Moving Your Body Moves Your Life

As a kid growing up in California, I loved to roller skate outside. About two years before my former husband and I separated, I began to feel drawn to a beautiful recreational park in Washington State called Green Lake. It had been years since I'd skated but my spirit nudged me to buy some Rollerblades and begin skating the 2.8 miles around the lake for exercise. We were living in the suburbs and it made no logical sense for me to drive thirty minutes each way, several times a week "just to work out." But I felt an inner *yes* pulling me, so I followed it.

After morning rounds on skates, I began exploring the neighborhoods around the lake. When it came time to seek out a new home, I knew I'd already found my neighborhood. Looking back, I realize that my soul was getting me acclimated to my new environment long before I was even aware that my marriage was ending and that I would be moving. I credit the lake's special healing energy for soothing me during the grieving period following my divorce, and for nourishing me as I built my coaching practice.

Your soul is always tuned in to what you need, even when your intellect says, "I'm stuck—I have no idea what to do!" My soul truly knew what it was doing when it guided me to this particular kind of exercise in this specific geographic area. Two things make me feel wonderfully alive and free: dancing and spending time in nature, preferably near a body of water. For me, rollerblading combines these two passions—it's like dancing in nature. When I'm feeling really loose and on a roll (no pun intended), I feel like I'm flying. Lately, I've added headphones and uplifting music to my skating routine, which really makes my spirit soar! How perfect then that my higher self would nudge me to return to my childhood passion of skating when my marriage began to unravel. It was exactly what I needed to move—*literally*—into the next chapter of my life.

On a purely practical level, moving your body is absolutely necessary to release daily stress and pent-up emotions. Joyful exercise strengthens your body—which then spills over, increasing your inner strength and courage to follow your heart. In the bigger picture, physical movement gets you unstuck on all levels: mental, emotional and spiritual.

Making a move moves you forward. As the late Gabrielle Roth wrote:

> When we move our bodies we shake up firmly rooted systems of thought, old patterns of behavior and emotional responses that just don't work anymore. Rhythm, breath, music and movement become tools for seeing, then freeing, the habits that hold us back. When we free the body, the heart begins to open. When the body and the heart taste freedom, the mind won't be far behind. And when we put the psyche into motion, it will start to heal itself. [11]

Move your body, shift your life.

 Exercise: *Loving Your Body*

Take a few moments to reflect on what you appreciate about your body and what it needs to thrive. One thing I appreciate about my body is …

What changes would make you feel more vital and alive …

- In your diet?

- In your water intake?

- In your exercise habits?

- In your sleep habits?

One of my favorite self-loving practices is a hot bath with sea salt and lavender essential oil. The sea salt clears away negative energy and the lavender oil is a natural relaxant.

- What is one body-nourishing thing that you already enjoy doing?

- What is one fun thing that you would like to do to love your body?

Feed Your Mind

Shortly before I had my first spiritual awakening, I remember browsing a great bookstore called *Third Place Books* with a dear friend. In the self-growth/spirituality section, a certain book caught my eye. With it's artful turquoise blue cover, *The 12 Secrets of Highly Creative Women*, by Gail McMeekin, called me to pick it up. I opened to Chapter One and read:

Acknowledging Your Creative Self

> Your creative self is alive and waiting for your invitation to evolve! Dare to embrace your creative self and manifest your dreams. Recognizing your creativity leads you into a life of self-expression, fulfillment, and contribution.[12]

I felt my mind open and my heart light up. That the book spoke to me was an understatement. Did the author write this just for me?! I wondered excitedly. I caressed the cover, flipped through the pages, and then set the delightful paperback back on display. "Sure, it's a cool book, but you don't really *need* it. Yes, it would be fun to read, but it's not a *necessity*." The inner critic had successfully elbowed her way into my enthusiasm. "And your husband definitely wouldn't approve." Then I heard the gavel fall: "You've been in school most of your life—you don't need another book!"

I told my friend I'd think about it. I browsed the store for what felt like an hour ruminating over the decision whether to give in to my "frivolous" desire and say yes. Clearly, I was still operating in an old way of thinking. My rational ego reminded me that I'd done my schooling—twelve years of high school, four years of college, and law school to boot—so clearly I did not need to invest in any more learning.

Sheesh, what was I thinking?! This is a good question, because the quality of your thoughts dictates the quality of your experience. And I wasn't having a happy one!

Fortunately, my heart won out and despite the critic's heavy-handed declarations, I gave myself permission. The pretty book came home with me. Devouring it filled my heart with inspiration, confidence, and courage to take the next step. I was reminded of my creative and artistic self's potential. Turns out that my education *wasn't* over for this lifetime. In some ways, it was just beginning. Unbeknownst to me at the time, I was taking baby steps in the school of soul-inspired living. Not long after, I enrolled in a life-changing, yearlong Expressive Arts Therapy (EAT) practitioner training. You never know when one tiny yes might tip the scales in favor of your soul's unfolding destiny.

Today I see the subject of nourishing the mind through wildly more alive and infinitely more inspired eyes. Your mind will keep expanding if you feed it with stimulating material that opens your consciousness and widens your perspective. Every day I read from at least one spiritually expansive book. I often listen to other authors' radio programs, and I play and sing high-consciousness music in my car, on my iPhone, and often when I'm getting ready for the day. I know now how vital it is to keep myself bathed in the consciousness that I desire to live and create from.

I also continue to nourish my mind with spiritual workshops, seminars, and retreats. I *love* to learn, and it's my joy to share and teach whatever I learn that lights me up. I used to think that I would reach the end of the consciousness learning curve. Ha—was I misinformed! Since your consciousness is unlimited, you are always growing and expanding into new ways of thinking, seeing, and being. Your soul yearns to be stimulated and fed with new, higher learning. As eternal spiritual warriors of the heart, we are continually unfolding into a higher vibrational octave.

Another thing about learning: because you are always growing, you can listen to the same exact program numerous times and pick up a new nugget each time. You can hear the same thing over and over from many teachers and one day, you hear it in a slightly different way, and you have an "aha!" that causes a breakthrough.

I agree with my former career coach, Rick Jarow, when he says that you don't actually show up to learn knowledge from your spiritual teachers as much as you go to receive energy downloads while in their presence. For example, at a workshop I may write down much of what my intellect heard, but it's the amazing feeling of awakened possibility that I am filling up on and taking home with me. I believe it is your spirit that feels called to attend a seminar because you sense that being in the facilitator's or speaker's company will wake you up and move you into this higher octave, helping you to remember the deeper truth about who you really are.

The intellect might say that you are going to learn and gain new information, but the mind cannot see the whole picture. I know that when I feel drawn to a particular teacher, I am poised for a new insight, revelation, or healing that will move me forward on my path. It rarely comes down to something they said. You also often meet new, like-minded soul friends and colleagues—an added bonus.

Thank goodness we are never finished evolving! My hunch is that if you are reading this, you too delight in your essence as an eternally growing spiritual warrior. Keep feeding your mind with inspirationally-nourishing materials and experiences. Celebrate this quest of the spirit. Say yes to your lust for life and learning. Say yes to your ever-evolving soul.

 Exercise: *Loving Your Mind*

Take a few moments to reflect on what your mind and intellect need to thrive.

For example:

I love to browse bookstores. I also enjoy researching spiritual ideas and questions on Google.

Now You:

- One thing I appreciate about my mind is …

- Does your mind receive enough stimulation, variety, and brain food? What changes would make you feel more vital and alive?

- One thing I do to nourish my mind is …

- Something I would like to do more of is …

Nourish Your Spirit

If I haven't already said it enough, I am a huge lover of beauty. I don't know if this has to do with my three years in law school studying for the bar exam and my concerted efforts to be a good, responsible lawyer for years afterward, but somewhere along the line I think I forgot how vital beauty was to my life force. I had forgotten that I was as much an artist as an attorney.

When I found myself in a circle of artists and healers in my Expressive Arts Therapy training, I rediscovered my passion for beauty in all forms. I started giving myself the time to be present so I could notice the everyday beauty in my midst.

I woke up to the gorgeousness of color, pattern, and texture in nature, fabrics, architecture, food, and art. Beauty shows up in almost every aspect of our sensual world—if we're looking for it. For example, I am in awe of the stunning beauty of flowers, so I always keep some in a vase in my office. I take umpteen photos of blooms, because their exquisite nature floors me.

What I know now, that I wasn't aware of when I practiced law, is this: your life is essentially a work of art, inspired by your soul's direction. In every moment, with every small step, you are choosing to nourish your soul—or not. And your soul needs beauty to thrive. Beauty, both appreciating it and creating it, is essential nourishment for your spirit.

I've always put a priority on beautifying my home spaces, but creating any sort of art just for fun was something I put on the back burner for years. I would get a soul nudge to paint a small picture, for example, but the inner critic would jump in before my spirit's excitement could take hold. "If you're not going to be a professional artist, and it's certainly too late for that, why play with color? Artists are *born* not made. Where is painting today going to get you?" Blah, blah, blah. This voice of the ego, edging our genius out, has such limited sight. The truth is that every nudge to do something small to nourish yourself *is* getting you somewhere worthwhile.

Right now, I am looking out the window of the Chocolati Café, where I am writing. I see fall trees covered with burnt orange leaves, their branches swaying in the wind as the dusky sky turns to purple and apricot. Taking the time to notice and appreciate this beauty reconnects me with my soul. The same is true for anything you love. Any activity that puts you in the zone, moves you into creative bliss, opens your heart, or lights you up counts. Doing what you love puts you in the flow where you have access to your inner clarity.

Research shows that creating with our hands reduces depression because of the mood-enhancing chemicals heart-to-hand activities produce.[13] People who knit and crochet vouch for working through issues as they go stitch by stitch. We often try to get clarity through the intellect, but our gut instincts are found in the belly. Using your hands drops your awareness down into your belly and heart. I love to cook and bake for this reason. When I need a solution, getting my hands in dough connects me with my inner wisdom, where my heart is waiting for me to consult it.

☀ Exercise: *Loving Your Spirit*

Take a few moments to reflect on what your spirit needs to thrive.

- One thing I appreciate about my spirit is …

- My spirit loves …

- What would bring my spirit more joy, fulfillment, adventure, or aliveness?

Cultivate a Daily Bliss Practice

I once offered a workshop called *Romancing your Inner Muse*. The soul, as I mentioned earlier, is like an inner romantic partner. It has to be lovingly invited in to your life. With our fast-paced world and never-ending to-do lists and responsibilities, we can't expect to hear the voice of our soul unless we consciously make room for it. That would be like expecting a romance to thrive without ever spending time with our beloved.

This inner lover gets us like no other. It wants to provide for our every need. It loves us unconditionally, knows us intimately, and wants us to have every desire and more. When expanded, the word *intimacy* yields *into-me-I-see*.

No one can know or love you better than your own soul. It pours its life force into your body to express the very aliveness you came to offer the world. When you take time to be intimate with your inner soul partner, you are rewarded with a depth of connection you may have never before known with a human partner. Diving into the deeper waters with your soul, you rise to the surface with a new recognition of yourself. Intimacy with others then becomes sweeter as well. Your connection to your soul generates a radiance that you cannot help but share with everyone.

A Daily Bliss Practice also rebalances you. During any practice, you connect not only with your spirit but also your emotions. You are brought closer to your feelings, so that you can meet them and release them. This is a cleansing process. The more you let go of, the more light and love can enter.

One of my favorite Daily Bliss Practices is rollerblading around Green Lake and singing along to spiritual music playing on my iPhone. Nearly every one of my senses is activated: I am moving my body, breathing in fresh air, listening to high-vibration tunes, and voicing my joy through song. It's like dancing on air. Any time you move your body, use your voice, take in beauty, and feed your mind with inspiration all at once, you can't help but elevate your mood.

Over the years, I have engaged in a wide variety of spiritual practices, ranging from journal writing to sitting meditation to running and art making. What they all have in common is an intention to connect to the inner guidance of my soul and Spirit. It doesn't matter what you do as long as it puts you in this flow of connection.

I meditate most days with an intention to feel and receive the love and guidance of Spirit. I often dance or walk with the same intention. As I introduced in Chapter Two, I also write to Spirit, asking for guidance and taking down the message that comes through. I cannot imagine living without these practices. They are strong anchors for me in living a spiritual path.

Whichever practice you choose, the key is your intention to connect. Set an intention to commune with your wise self, the voice of your heart and soul, before your practice. Voice this to yourself before dancing or walking, or write it down when you sit down to journal or write to Spirit.

I invite you to start anywhere—just start! Choose a practice that feels the most appealing now.

If you decide to journal, writing three 8.5 X 11 pages or twenty minutes per day works well. I have found my journaling often begins with a 'dumping' of my emotions and thoughts, like taking out the garbage. After this release, I start to feel lighter and my inspiration has space to enter. Around the end of page two or the start of page three, I begin to feel more uplifted. A new idea or insight may flow in. I continue journaling until I feel calm and at ease, ready to move into the day.

You may also want to choose a certain time of day, like morning or before bed, to establish your journaling routine. Creating space in your calendar will support you to show up and connect with your soul. The more you show up at your appointed time, the more you'll feel your soul showing up for you.

Now you:

The Daily Bliss Practice I would like to create is:

I am committing to do this practice:

_____ in the morning

_____ in the evening

Or, write in the time of day you will do your practice:

_____

9

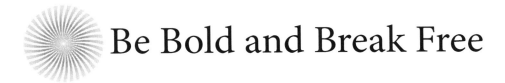

Be Bold and Break Free

And the trouble is, if you don't risk anything, you risk even more.

~ Erica Jong

Dear Spirit,

I step now into your arms and feel your embrace melt me into the deepest expression of your infinite love. I relax fully into you. I know that you love me beyond human reason ... beyond love as I can fathom it. Show me in neon lights that I am supported in ways so miraculous—ways that I have not yet even imagined. Let me swiftly get used to feeling this wonderful. As I do, turn me into the next brilliant hue of who I came here to be. Turn me into the most courageous expression of your bright light. Make me into courage itself.

~ A Journal Entry

Last spring, my friend Dave and I got stuck on a major thoroughfare in Seattle called the 520-bridge, en route to an evening out dancing. On this two-lane bridge in the middle of Lake Washington, traffic was at a standstill, making a long stream of headlights, with cars backed up as far as we could see. People even began to get out to discern the cause. Dave, who was driving, began to mutter under his breath that we might miss the band altogether.

Dave is my prayer partner, so we have periodic talks about what we want to manifest in our lives. I have shared with him my heart's desire to release my remaining shyness and say yes to expressing my full authentic nature—to live a life some call *living out loud*. For instance, I want to free myself to go out on the dance floor even if I am the only one—even if my dance partner is sitting this one out. Dancing by myself? Easier said than done. I hear my free-spirited soul saying, "I love this song! Let's go!" But my fearful ego resists just enough to keep me in my chair.

Just before Dave and I left my house, I had voiced my intention to let go of my fears even more and follow my spirit. Now here we were, still stuck on the bridge. Drivers began turning off their engines. I was beginning to feel discouraged, thinking we might not get to dance tonight at all. Then the famous Rolling Stones tune "You Can't Always Get What You Want" came flooding into my head, reminding me that maybe I wasn't getting what I wanted, but I could still go for what I *needed*.

What's stopping us from dancing right here, right now? I thought. What's the worst that could happen—people assuming I'm crazy, ridiculing or making fun of me? Their criticism was unlikely to go further than the privacy of their own mind or car. Who is going to accost a happy dancer? All of this went through my mind in a split second as I felt my ego rebel with, "Noooo!" But in that moment of desire to break through my comfort zone, I felt a wonderful rush of possibility.

"Will you crank up the radio and dance with me?!" I turned to Dave.

"Right here?" he responded with a tiny bit of yes in his voice.

"Yes! It will be great!" I enthused.

Dave put his hand on the dial and turned up the music.

And we did it.

With a long line of headlights beaming right on us, we got out and danced on the bridge. I almost couldn't believe I was doing it, but I felt exhilarated.

I was breaking free!

Freeing ourselves always means stepping into unknown territory. And the unknown naturally triggers fear—it's how our brains are wired. I know from taking other risks, however, that exhilarated fear is a sure sign of yes! The presence of fear along with excitement is my soul telling me that a big reward awaits me on the other side of going for it.

I know that when I receive an inspired impulse, this is my soul saying, "Wake up!" The soul's essence is like a sparkling diamond with unlimited facets of light-filled expression. When I feel an inner nudge that comes with exhilarated fear, a new facet of my soul is ready to break through and become real—to show up in the world as more of me.

We can imagine what would make our lives better and what would make the world a better place, but if we don't honor our impulses to move on the divine direction we receive, we'll suffer for it. This is what poets refer to as the *unlived life*. We may not recognize it as such. We might just feel restless or blame our job or lack of money or other people. Or we lose hope, and the passion of feeling truly alive eludes us day in and day out. Life feels life-less, because it *lacks us*.

When you hold back, you are keeping your greatest life—your destiny—at arms length.

On the bridge that night, in the pitch dark, surrounded by a great expanse of water and with hundreds of car headlights shining on us, I felt something bigger than fear or my own inhibitions cheering me on. I felt the possibility that going for it might inspire *others* to let go, and somewhere in their lives feel the fear and do it anyway.

Imagining all of us breaking free from our self-imposed cages lights me up because it fuels my larger, passionate vision for humanity. Imagine how life would be if we *all* said yes to those little soul nudges to break through the ego's resistance. When one of us takes a risk, our yes gives others permission to do the same. We feel their wind, catch it … and fly.

Here's the thing: in this dance of life, every new step expands you and opens you up to the power of your true self. Just one more baby step outside of your comfort zone lets you be just a little more true to your spirit's essence. Baby steps build momentum and soon you have the confidence to dance into a greater vision of your life than you could have imagined possible.

Most important, the extent to which you say yes to your inner nudges of possibility determines the level of passion and aliveness you feel in your life. No one else is going to give you permission!

And there's a cost to saying no. If you ignore or suppress the nudges, you know, inside, that you're not fully showing up for yourself. You have fallen out of integrity with your soul. When you don't dare to break out of the preset molds handed down to you and let yourself grow and expand, dis-ease expands instead. If the promise of inspired possibility doesn't work to pull you toward your destiny, your soul will not give up. It will get your attention in other ways, sometimes resulting in painful emotional or physical symptoms. The soul is less concerned about how you awaken. It is, however, intent that you awaken.

Freeing Yourself to Live Out Loud

I advocate moving gently into freeing yourself to live out loud. I began by noticing the "Wouldn't it be great if … " whispers of my soul. Like, "Wouldn't it be great if everyone felt free to dance anywhere?" "Wouldn't life be more fun if we all felt more liberated to express our true selves?"

If I wanted to change this in the world, I needed to first shift it within myself. I can't expect society to change its cultural rules if I'm not willing to first free myself from my own inner rules. Each of us, one by one evolving our individual lives, leads to evolution in our families and our communities, and eventually ripples out to the planet.

It's okay to use training wheels until you graduate to saying yes to your bigger vision. Listen to your soul's whispers. Do the next small thing that brings you joy.

I love the way the late John O'Donohue so beautifully describes the dream of your soul as your "secret signature." [14] I imagine your secret signature etched in gold on the mysterious canvas of your soul's essence. You will find your signature, your golden essence, by listening to the substance of your spirit's whispers. "Come out." "Go ahead, just do it." "Come on out, just a little bit more."

I invite you to give in to these small intuitive invitations of delight and daring. Coming out becomes easier when you're attuned to your inner world and what makes you come alive. Fully inhabiting your inner world readies you to be an exuberant, full-out player in your outer world.

Begin with a clear intention—an intention to be mindful of your own needs and authentic desires. Often we're so busy doing our regular routines we have no clue what would make us feel more alive and free. If we tune in and ask, our childlike, creative self will always give us the answer. Common responses from our inner kid include: "I want to have fun! I want to play. I want to feel loved. I need to feel safe." With encouragement and support, we can give the child what she needs, and begin to see delightful results—even breakthroughs.

Notice, too, your "coulda-woulda-shouldas." I heard the inner nudge of, "Dance anywhere! Even if no one else is doing it," a number of times before I finally broke free. After dancing on the bridge, I felt high for days afterward. I'm sure I also looked more radiant—an added bonus!

Of course, I didn't dance free alone. Having Dave's support made a huge difference. He danced with me for a minute or so and stopped. Which was okay. He'd supported me in lifting off so I had enough wind beneath my wings to keep flying. From there, my soul took over as my dance partner.

Dave's pause also provided an opportunity. He snapped a photo so I could share my "coming out" on Facebook. I almost didn't post it. "People will think you're showing off," cautioned the inner critic. Then I felt the positive whoosh of Spirit's encouragement: "Let that go. Others will be inspired … share your enthusiasm!" So I did, and I received a huge, enthusiastic response. People's likes and comments confirmed for me that when we step out, it fuels others with joy and courage as well—courage that others can borrow and leverage to fly free themselves.

Taking this step gave me the confidence to do the next scary thing.

Not long after that evening, another impulse made itself known. I was heading down to Green Lake to rollerblade, and my inner guidance prompted, "Bring your music and ear buds." Well it's almost impossible for me to listen to music and hold back singing. I love to sing as much as I love to dance, but in our culture, unless you have a performance-quality voice, public singing is not encouraged. People tend to look at you very strangely—they think you're odd, eccentric, a show-off or … (you fill in the blank). "Sing anyway! This is too much fun—rollerblading and singing to your favorite tunes. It's too much fun to say no to, just because you fear other people's 'disapproval.'" The exhilarated fear was cheering me on again. "Okay," I thought, "I've already said yes to coming out all the way, I can't stop now."

A couple of month's later, I was offered the chance to host my own talk radio show, which I named *Just Say Yes!* Having my own show had been a dream of mine, but I hadn't yet felt ready. Now I see that dancing on the bridge and singing my heart out on skates were my soul's way of preparing me to come out and guide others on the radio.

The soul always knows how to lead you to your next greatest expression. The ego can't show you the way because its modus operandi is always about playing it safe. Even if you have ambitious goals, Spirit may still have something even more expansive in mind for you.

If you're very fortunate, at some point you wake up and realize that there's more to life than what you had originally planned. It's not about having more or spending more, it's about living your larger purpose. To contribute, experience, and express more than you originally thought you were here for calls for a bigger plan: the soul's plan. Soul nudges are the inspired self's way of revealing the next step in your divine destiny.

I encourage you to just say yes to those little nudges you've been getting to take a risk. Your yes will infuse you with a new, exhilarated sense of inner freedom. You will be infused with more of your soul's authentic power and radiant light. You will also be proud of yourself for feeling the fear and doing it anyway.

Life wants us to be true to our guiding genius. That's how we come alive.

Exercise: *Taking the Risk to Soar*

Give yourself a few moments to reflect. Even if you're not sure of your truth, your soul knows! I invite you to answer the following questions quickly. Take a few deep breaths and relax. Drop down into your heart and connect to your inner guidance.

Without trying to think it up, let your heart respond. Speak the questions out loud and notice what comes up. Don't censor your answers. Write down what comes to you even if you are sure you would "never do it."

- If I gave myself permission to feel full-throttle joy, I would …

- I don't usually act on it, but sometimes I have the wild impulse to …

- If I didn't care what anyone else thought, I would …

Taking action …

- What one small step are you willing to take to come out just a little bit more?

- When you take action, be sure to document and celebrate your wins!

The Courage to Belong to Ourselves

A while back I attended a silent meditation retreat led by two internationally known spiritual teachers for whom I have tremendous admiration and respect. When they facilitate a workshop or talk, their radiant love is palpable. My spirit lit up at the thought of meeting them in person so I could share how much their work had helped me on my path. I flew to California for the event, filled with excitement. I was thrilled to be spending four days with such passionate and powerful leaders.

We all silently ate our meals together in the dining commons, which meant that most of our communication happened exclusively through body language—through our smiles and eyes. Each day, I attempted to connect in this way with one of the teachers, but she did not return my glances or smiles. I noticed how much it bothered me inside. Not only was I disappointed that we might not meet as I'd hoped, but my ego began making up stories like, "Maybe she doesn't like me; maybe she has no interest in meeting me."

As much as I wanted to connect with her, what mattered more was my desire to enjoy my retreat—to feel happy and free. Thinking about her response to me was getting in the way of my happiness. I took my intention to feel free into my meditation and received clarity. Why was I disappointed? I realized that I wanted her to see and acknowledge my presence. I also wanted her to like me.

It didn't take me long to see that letting go of my need for my beloved mentor to like me was the inner work of the retreat for me. On the last day, we had a sunrise ritual with a bonfire ceremony. Each of us took turns releasing what no longer served us into the fire. I released my need for my teacher's, and anyone else's, approval. And how tremendously freeing it was! It brought me back to my authentic spirit: an unlimited being who deserves to feel joyful and loved no matter how someone else is relating to me.

Needing someone else's approval, love, or acceptance is the opposite of liberating. It binds and restricts us. If we're relying on outside validation, we won't feel free to take the next risk to be fully ourselves.

Being attached to how another is behaving toward us is a call for self-love. We all forget from time to time that no matter what anyone else thinks of us, we are enough—*more* than enough. We forget that we have a much deeper reservoir of acceptance within us: the true source of love—the soul. When we forget, we can go back to the truth of who we are, back to pleasing ourselves, back to loving and nurturing our creative desires.

This is how we practice belonging to ourselves. Belonging to ourselves gives us the courage to say yes to our souls' impulses to step out and become more real, regardless of what anyone else thinks.

Claiming Your Place in the World

I remember in high school wanting to be "popular." I was on the shy side, and though I was friendly with many, I always preferred to have deeper conversations that went below the surface with a few. I had a wonderful group of friends, but only a small group of people knew me intimately. Every year, around the time yearbooks were being compiled, our school would have end-of-the-year competitions for the Best and Most awards: Best Looking, Most Likely to Succeed, Most Popular, etc. Each class voted on the nominees. The winners would be featured in yearbook photo spreads. Deep down, I yearned to be nominated for something. It never happened. On some level, I felt invisible.

Years later, I wanted to heal any sense of not enough-ness stemming from my childhood years. When I reflected on feeling unrecognized in high school, I had a revelation. The truth was that it was never my heart's desire to engage on a daily basis with a lot of people, as I saw many of the award-winning kids doing. I was fulfilled with the smaller number of close relationships that I had. I did want to be recognized for my gifts and talents, but I wasn't at all interested in doing anything to gain my schoolmates' favor to win the Best or the Most of anything.

Sometimes not being chosen by others makes you feel like you don't fit in. In fact, you can go through much of your life trying to feel like you truly belong in this body, in this biological family, or in the culture you grew up in. Sometimes you might wonder if you *were* dropped off on your parents' doorstep by a stork, you feel that different from everyone else!

Underneath the desire to belong is the desire to feel confident and at home in your own skin. What you really want is to feel free to be your true self so you can let go, have fun, and shine. It can take a while to really know in your bones that your presence here serves an important purpose beyond anyone else choosing you—that your true place of belonging is with Spirit, with your soul.

The truth is, *your soul has chosen you*. This is your real home. Once you awaken to this truth, you can relax and feel at home anywhere. You can feel free to fully come out.

Claiming your place in the world, really saying yes to being your true self, insecurities and all, is a heroic act.

The following meditation will strengthen your connection with your inner wise guide. Forging a bond with your soul will heighten your ability to discern its nudges. It will also bring the healing experience of feeling unconditionally loved. This love is your birthright.

 Meditation: *Connect with Your Inner Soul Partner*

I invite you now to relax and close your eyes. Take in a nice deep breath and release it. Continue to breathe. Breathe in peace, and let go of everything else. Breathe in peace, and let go of the rest. You are safe. You are protected. You are divinely guided. No matter what is happening in your life right now, all is truly well. In the big picture of life, you are on track.

Begin to relax your body starting at the top of your head. Feel the sensations in your forehead and your scalp. Relax the muscles in your face. As you continue to breathe, let your jaw relax and drop open. Soften the back of your neck. Let your shoulders drop down. Soften your belly. Breathe into your heart center. You may want to put one or both hands on your heart. Connect to any emotions you are feeling right now. Without judgment, here in the sacred space of your mind and heart, name the emotion or emotions to yourself. Feel the sensation and let it go.

As you breathe, you begin to feel more and more connected to your own wise self. To the voice of your spirit. I invite you to connect to an intention. If you could choose any quality or emotion that you want to create your life with, what would you choose? Allow your heart to give you the word. For example, *I am calm. I am confident. I am happy.*

I invite you now to bring this intention with you into a peaceful and beautiful place in nature. Imagine that you are walking along a tree-lined pathway. You see a gate, covered in fragrant white blooms. You walk through this gate into a sanctuary for your spirit. This is a place of your own creation. Your own imagination, your own spirit, has brought you here. This is a place of power for you. Feel it now. Feel the vibration of this sanctuary. It is vibrating to the high frequency of your intention. Where intention goes, energy flows. There are no accidents. Your spirit has brought you here for a healing, for an important message, to move you forward on your path.

Give thanks now for being here at the perfect time in your destiny. You are so guided. You are so on track.

Look around this beautiful place in nature and locate a tree—there is a tree here that is calling to you—that is beckoning you to it. A powerful tree that is extending its spirit of love to you. Allow yourself to go to this tree now. Stand up against it and feel your spine connected to the tree's trunk. Feel the energy of this tree moving up from the base of your spine to the top of your head, rejuvenating you. The thriving nature of mother earth, replenishing your energy. And here in this power place, with your spine connected to the tree, I invite you to connect with Spirit.

Very soon a guide, a Spirit guide, in the image of your higher self or soul will appear. Very soon you will begin to sense and feel this presence—the presence of your inner guidance and your own wise self.

Imagine, sense, and feel now that a thick warm fog is rolling in, just momentarily obscuring your view of your sanctuary. As the fog rolls in, you begin to feel more and more of this presence. You do not see it yet, but you sense it. When I count to six, the fog will begin to roll out again. And you will sense or see your own wise self in front of you. One. Two. Three. Coming closer now. You are beginning to feel it even more. Four. Moving closer now. It may come in the form of a color or sound. Or the feeling of a loving presence. It may or may not show up in the form of a being. Just trust what comes. Five. The fog is now lifting. Six. You now see, feel, sense, or hear the presence of your own wise self—your inner soul partner—your spirit. Celebrate … rejoice … embrace this visit from your spirit.

Your inner soul partner has a gift for you. Imagine now that whatever presence has come to you, at your feet they have placed a gift. Perhaps there's a treasure box covered by a cloth. Look down and notice what is there. Lift off the cover. See your gift. If you knew, what would it be? Some things are true even if we do not believe them. Allow your imagination to make this gift clearer to you. Know that even if you see nothing now, powerful seeds have been planted … seeds that will bring clarity in the days, weeks and months to come.

For now, send gratitude to the presence of your spirit. Embrace this presence with love and say goodbye for now. Remember that you can return to this place in your imagination whenever you wish.

Begin to walk out of your sanctuary, imagining that you are taking the pathway back to the space that you started from. Begin to gently transition back into an awareness of your physical body. Come back to your breath, and gently move until you are fully back. When you are ready, return to present time.

You may want to journal about your meditation experience. Our spirit often speaks to us in metaphor. Images may have a symbolic rather than literal meaning. Write down any message(s) or gifts you received from your higher self in this visualization. Your own inner guidance will tell you what it wants you to glean from your experience. Trust what you receive.

10

 # Protect Your Passions

Don't wait around for other people to be happy for you. Any happiness you get, you've got to make for yourself.

~Alice Walker

Give yourself tender self-care, no matter what is happening. Remember that you rock, even when it doesn't feel that way. You are infinitely loved.

~ A Journal Entry

As Eleanor Roosevelt said, "What others think of me is none of my business." *Our business is to create the most fulfilling, luscious life that radiates such love and lust for being here that we can't help but be magnetic to our hearts' desires.

As inventors of a great life, we are often pioneering a new way of being. This will inspire many to say yes and free themselves. But some will not necessarily understand or feel excited about the changes we are celebrating. Our newfound expression may inadvertently make them feel uncomfortable or afraid. This is because when we free ourselves, it often reminds others of the places where they have not yet freed *themselves.*

When I sing out loud while skating around Green Lake, for example, I am aware that I am going outside the norm. I realize that some people may not appreciate my less than perfect singing voice. Others may want to sing too, but they haven't yet given themselves permission to go outside the lines of how "most people" act.

I have to consciously remind myself that I don't want to be "normal" anyway. By contrast, I want to live in a world where everyone feels free to sing in public, just as birds do. As Oliver Wendell Holmes said, "If only the best birds sang, how silent the woods would be." Besides that, "normal" reflects the world we live in right now. If we want to create a better world, we have to be willing to innovate our own "new normal."

It's not always easy to find your true voice. Most of us have spent much of our lives trying to please others or "be nice." So we keep quiet about our needs, desires, or feelings in order to be liked or accepted. We may feel afraid to speak up for fear of another's reaction. Your own truth is right there inside of you, but it can get camouflaged by negative emotions that drain your energy unless you feel and move through these emotions.

Becoming aware of when you are emotionally triggered is a powerful bridge to finding your truth. When someone comes along and pushes your buttons, they are actually acting as an angel in disguise. It sounds odd, but it's true. Even naysayers can become the bridge that returns you to your true self.

For example, I once had a regular reader of my blog who sent me a slew of emails criticizing my writing. Her messages were what I call "crazy making." [15] Crazy making is another person's unhelpful, undermining, or just plain attacking behavior that pulls you away from your inspired focus. Always distracting, crazy making includes criticism, couched as "feedback," that feels intrusive or intentionally hurtful.

The gift of other people's crazy making behavior is that it gets your attention so that you can heal what is coming up. Feeling distracted or emotionally upset is a call to go inside and see what you need—to put your focus on your own happiness instead of on pleasing others.

Anger or hurt feelings are also a sign that you're ready to stand even more firmly in your truth. To be authentically successful, you need to know what you stand for. You need to be willing to speak your truth. You can begin with telling *yourself* the truth. You don't have to share your truth with anyone else until you're ready. The first step is to create a safe and comforting place to express your emotions, needs, and desires. Writing down how you feel is a great start. You can do it in a lovely journal or a basic spiral notebook. I use spiral notebooks because I go through so many. If you want a prompt, begin with this simple sentence:

I feel _____ about _____.

For example, *I feel depressed about this constant gray weather.* Or, *I feel lousy about the way my mother spoke to me on the phone.*

I like to think of this as a clearing process. It's not about thinking anything up. It's about naming your feelings, acknowledging and feeling them, and then letting them go.

Imagine that by putting your pen to paper and dumping your feelings and thoughts on the page, you are doing the equivalent of taking out the garbage. In so doing, you are making room for your dreams.

Here's the beauty of this process: after a certain period, you'll begin to observe what is you, ranting and releasing, and you, voicing the truth of your spirit. You'll begin to recognize the difference between the inner critic and the infinitely wise part of you. You'll feel your heart light up when you flash on a piece of inner guidance. You will begin to see the pattern of what your heart really wants.

Becoming clear about your truth builds your inner strength. Your inner strength is like a diving board you can spring off of to take the next step: courageously sharing with others.

If you're living your path with commitment to yourself—with gusto—you will at times feel like the lone voice at the top of the mountain. Invariably, some won't like what you have to say or what you have done, and they'll let you know.

Don't let the naysayers pull you off your path.

You may feel hurt and wonder where all of your supporters are. That's when it's helpful to call a friend who has your back and say, "Tell me again what you see in me that I'm not seeing right now." That's when you can go back to your soul, to your inner soul partner, and get the love, support, and guidance you need to keep going. This is the dance of the spiritual warrior—the dance of you, being the hero of your life.

You Matter

Years ago, I became accustomed to what I call *overgiving*. I saw my role as nurturer and caretaker of our family, and I took pride in creating a beautiful home and putting my kids' needs first. But not just my kids—virtually everyone I knew. If someone needed something, I could always do my own work later, I figured. I was used to prioritizing the needs of others. And everyone else was used to me showing up when they needed me.

One night I had this dream:

> I am checking into a comfortable hotel with lovely amenities. When I open the door to my room, however, I find to my great surprise that it is occupied. My room is teaming with people—a high school baseball team—to be exact. The ten or so teenaged boys in my room just played a tournament, and my room looks and smells like a boys' locker room. I ask them to leave and they say it's *their* room. They do offer me a tiny space in one corner of the room to sleep and put my things. When I return to the front desk to report the obvious mishap, they tell me they have no other rooms and that "This is the way we do things here." I am angry that the hotel expects me to share my previously reserved room. They are clearly not honoring my need for privacy.

The dream recurred two more times before I got it. My soul was attempting to show me that I didn't have to share all of my space! The dream's message was clear: honor your own needs and create some healthy boundaries.

I asked myself, In what area(s) of my life am I not honoring my need for room and privacy? Where am I not allowing *me* to take up space?

The great thing about these kinds of observational questions is that they get answered! The soul—your wise inner guidance—is partnering with you to shine light on your patterns and ways of being that aren't supporting your most joyful life.

For example, I noticed that if one of my adult daughters called me, I would drop whatever I was doing and answer the phone even if I was focused on an important deadline. If a friend wanted to get together, I would do my best to accommodate their schedule, rather than pause to think about the best times for me. I began to see that my own habit of considering everyone else's preferences before my own was draining my energy and completely filling up my "living space." I had very little time or room left for my own creative projects or dreams. I noticed months and then a year go by when I wasn't writing my book, even though I felt inspired. Something was clearly off.

I began a simple practice that helped immensely to free up my time. When opportunities and requests came my way, I would pause and check in with myself before responding. Imagine that! I didn't have to get back to the person that minute. I gave myself a little breathing room. I started to factor my needs and desires into the equation of my decisions. What did *I* want to do? Did I really want to say yes, or was I showing up out of obligation or duty?

I began to say no … unless my answer was an enthusiastic yes!

At first, I got pushback from those closest to me. I was told more than once that I was being "selfish." That stung a little, because I was still identifying with being a nurturer who drops everything for those she loves. In my mind at the time, "selfish" meant not showing up as a caring or loving person. This wasn't true about me. I care very much about my daughters, my family, my friends, clients and community, and the world.

Now I have a new definition of selfish: caring about the self. Yourself. Being selfish is loving yourself enough to put energy and presence into your own creativity and dreams. It is loving yourself enough to say yes to *you*.

All living things thrive within a safe and nurturing home environment. Plants need good soil, water, and light to grow. We need homes that give us comfort and a sense of sanctuary and belonging. Our hearts' desires and dreams, too, need a safe and roomy container in which to germinate and flourish. They need protection from outside forces that may interfere. The following exercise will help you protect what's important to you and say no to what is not. It will also support you in creating boundaries around what matters most to you. It will serve as a powerful visual map of what you need to flourish and thrive.

I invite you to create a Yes Map.

Exercise: *The Magic of a Yes Map*

The purpose of this exercise is to help you clarify all that you desire to say yes to in your life, and all that you do not. It asks you to draw a circle around what matters most to you in order to protect it with a clear and conscious boundary.

My approach to this exercise is inspired by a Native American medicine shield. A medicine shield is thought to invoke both spiritual and physical protection by the native. Traditionally, it is decorated with power symbols or objects of personal significance. The act of creating a medicine shield is a practice of putting your desires into the world and asking for divine assistance. This ritual also sends a powerful message to the subconscious mind, clarifying your intentions and desires.

Create a Yes Map

I like to create mine on a piece of large poster board so I have plenty of room. I use colored markers because color is more fun and makes your map more vibrant and fun to look at daily.

Before beginning, I invite you to relax and breathe and let your inner child or muse come out and play in the process. The muse loves a candle and music too! Open to your imagination. Let yourself have fun making your Yes Map.

- On your poster board or paper, draw a large circle with crayons or markers. This circle represents all that your heart desires and all that you are inviting into your world.

- *Inside your circle*: write down everything you desire. What do you absolutely need to feel happy, safe, secure, and fully alive? Include your work, relationships, creativity, finances, health, home, play, travel, and adventure.

The world is your oyster here. You get to decide what to put in your circle! Don't limit yourself to your "current reality" or what you think you know how to manifest. Open to the possibility that by putting your desires on your map, you are opening to receiving them in your life. You are also activating and attracting all the support and resources you need to call them into your reality.

I include what I need to feel good and energized. For example, daily exercise, including walks, yoga and rollerblading. I also include what I desire but don't yet have. For example, I may desire a lucrative book-publishing contract. I have no idea how this will come about, or whether the essence of my dream will show up in this form. Still, it lights up my heart to imagine receiving it, so I put it in my circle.

- *Outside your circle*, you will include a different category of desires. On the outside of your circle, write down what you are willing to have in your life… *by invitation only.*

  For example:

  Outside my circle I have written …

  By invitation only: *I am willing to receive helpful, constructive feedback.*

I encourage you to hang your Yes Map someplace you will see it daily. Mine is in my office. Some like to put theirs on the refrigerator. You are imprinting your subconscious mind with your preferences and desires, and the subconscious mind learns by repetition. The more it sees what you desire, the more it gets the message to draw these things and experiences into your life.

Enjoy the process of creating your Yes Map. Remember to mark and celebrate your successes when you say no and make more room for you.

Readiness Plus Action Equals Momentum

I love the mystery of how the soul propels us forward to reach, stretch, and take chances that bring us growth and expansion. So much magic can happen when we choose to actively partner with the soul and activate the courage to go beyond what we've done before. Taking action gets our momentum going. Momentum starts a flow. Once we're back in the flow, creating change feels easier.

A few weeks ago I began working with a new client named Mark. His stress level was so high that he'd been seeing a health counselor. He was feeling trapped in his job of fifteen years. He felt unappreciated by his supervisor, disliked most of his duties, and was experiencing fear and anxiety daily at work. He had almost no time to enjoy his family, and was feeling especially discouraged to have gained back some of the weight he'd released earlier.

I asked him about his passion. He lit up talking about his love of writing. "On the side," he had published several books. He wanted nothing more than to move on from his job and become a full-time professional writer.

Mark was ready to take action to cause a shift in his world from the inside out. Since he wasn't ready to leave his job until he found a better one, we talked about how he could show up for work, the work he had grown to dislike, in a new way.

The hardest work anyone will ever do is to change their attitude about a situation they desperately want to leave. Mark would say he had no choice, and it's true that his physical, emotional, and mental health were all getting his attention with stressful symptoms. Still, it takes courage to claim your part in making yourself miserable and be willing to do your best to turn things around.

Mark was ready to open his heart and accept "what was" at work until a more suitable opportunity came along. He also agreed to take exquisite care of himself in the meantime, and to affirm daily on the drive to work, "I am empowered and feeling safe." He left our first session feeling more energized with a new perspective.

When he came back for our second session two weeks later, Mark seemed a lot more relaxed, and he had a big smile on his face. "I've been getting up at 5 a.m. and working out with my wife every morning. I've already lost five pounds," he reported with joy. "My job is still tough, but I've applied for another one, and a dream job opened up that I'm applying for as well." I could see that an inner shift had happened. He had the wind back in his sails.

What shifted? Mark went out of his comfort zone. He had applied for different jobs before, but hadn't followed up with the potential employer or asked his contacts to put in a good word for him. This time he was more proactive. He took a risk, asked for support, and got it. He came away with a letter of recommendation from a best-selling author for his "dream job."

Mark made the choice to stop seeing himself as a victim of a lousy situation that had no way out. He stopped blaming his boss and others whose behavior was causing him stress. He began giving himself the nourishment and support he needed. And he mustered the courage to take some action. With each new move, he empowered and freed himself to say yes to his heart's vision for his life.

Remember: Whatever is happening in your life, keep calm and carry on. Breathe, and breathe again. Don't let the naysayers pull you off of your path. Taking action gets things moving. Movement gets you back in the flow.

What is one action you could take to get back in your flow?

11

Answering the Call

Only passions, great passions, can elevate the soul to great things.

~Denis Diderot

Remember, where change lurks, wisdom is yours for the asking. When the way you've always done life seems to be unraveling, your wise self is calling you to claim your hero or heroine status and say yes to a new adventure. Bravely step forward. It's impossible to go back, and soon you will realize that you wouldn't want to anyway.

~ A Journal Entry

It was November 2001. As a soul tribe of thirteen women, we were close to completing a yearlong training in Expressive Arts Therapy (EAT). Our fearless leader and facilitator, Jane Goldberg, sent us out into the woods. We were directed to find a "magic implement" to assist in the hero's journey of answering the call of our soul.

Here's the scenario Jane gave us: Imagine that you receive a phone call from Spirit, God, your higher power, soul, or inner guidance. It's a big deal. God is on the line. Calling you about your destiny, giving you a clear vision, or at the very least, direction on the next step on your path. You are being asked to report for duty—to answer the call of your soul and say yes! Very exciting! Who wouldn't want to get a call from God with easy-to-understand instructions on what to do next?

"But there's a catch," Jane said. "Like every hero's journey, along the way you will encounter what feels like an insurmountable obstacle. To move through it, you will need extraordinary help and support." Hence, her assignment to go into the forest to find a physical object that would serve as a magic power implement. With this implement, she explained, we could invoke the hidden powers of the soul to move through anything that showed up to block our progress.

I loved our mission. Akin to a vision quest, we were being asked to set the intention to be clearly guided to the just-right tool that would move us forward. My heart stirred with excitement. Then the ego stepped in and voiced its skepticism. My next thought was, "Seriously? What implement, besides a stick, rock, or pile of pine needles, am I going to find in this relatively small grove of trees adjacent to the retreat center?"

Jane assured us that she hadn't planted any suitable magical objects in the wilderness. But she knew from years of doing this exercise with groups that for every seeker, the right implement always makes itself known.

And this is what I love about the power of intention. When we set a clear intention to find something, the subconscious mind puts out feelers to locate it—even when the ego or inner critic believes it is ridiculously improbable. As soon as we open our hearts to the possibility of finding the perfect something, we've created a portal for it to materialize.

We all bundled up and ventured out, one by one, into the cold and rainy forest. For me, it happened almost immediately. Barely peeking out from a pile of fallen pine branches and cedar boughs was a slightly worn and muddied fluorescent green tennis ball. I was amazed to spot my treasure so quickly. I had no idea how it might help me overcome any obstacles, but my heart's warm delight in discovering the Green Machine, as I came to call it, told me this was absolutely my implement! Feeling that *just know* feeling, I scooped it up and brought it back to our yurt, trusting that its purpose would reveal itself later.

Now it was time to let our souls do the talking. We each found a cozy spot to begin writing and let our imaginations roll. "If you were to get a call from God (or the like) sending you on a heroic adventure," Jane said, "what would you want to hear? Where would you be directed? Listen to your heart—it will tell you."

My heart and Spirit spoke to me in this way:

> *Hello, Betsy, this is God. Your soul and I want you to move forward on your vision to become a spiritual teacher. This is your vision and it is happening. Your first stop: you need to take an adventure. Sell the old 4X4 jeep that is saddling you with big repairs. Get yourself the new red Honda with the sunroof you've that been eyeing. Take a road trip to that beautiful place, Santa Fe, you've been yearning to see. Bring along your favorite tunes. You will love being on the open road. You will see a lot along the way that will open your heart, revitalize you, and reveal more. First step: buy the car.*

So I did. The day we picked up the new license plates, I got a little hunch that felt like a whoosh of joyful possibility moving through my heart. "If the plates' letters have anything to do with New Mexico," I said to my girls and former husband, "this car is meant to drive us to Santa Fe!" We all chuckled, and my daughters jumped out of the car to see if their mom's wish would be fulfilled. I read the letters out loud: "NMC," which immediately translated in my mind to **N**ew **M**exico **C**ar.

> *I felt another whoosh of yes! I couldn't have received a more crystal clear sign from the Universe.*

Every new possibility, vision, or soul calling begins with a seed of desire. To move forward and co-create your future, you must first allow yourself to dream. Dreaming is the realm of the imagination. Anything wonderful in your life began as a spark of possibility in your imagination. This is how you connect with your creative yearnings, your soul's potential, and the blueprint of your destiny.

✳ Exercise: *Imagining the Call*

For this exercise, you'll need a few sheets of paper and a pen. You might want to use colored markers—just because imagining in color is fun! As we did in our EAT training, find a cozy spot where you won't be interrupted, and light a candle if you wish. Intend, as you put your lit match to the wick, that you are connecting with your creative flow. As you light the candle, you might affirm, "I am now connecting with my imagination and the inner voice of my soul."

Take a few deep breaths now and relax. Soften the muscles in your face, relax your jaw, and let your shoulders drop down. Let yourself play in your writing, without any expectations of what will come through. Often when we journey into the imaginary realm, we find surprises. Be open to what comes. Remember that you don't have to act on anything you sense if you don't want to. You are in charge of your own destiny. For now, just relax, open up, and let the playful kid in you have some fun as you imagine the following scenario:

Imagine that you have just received a phone call from God, Spirit, your soul, or your wise inner guidance. You are being called to action with an idea, inspiration, vision, possibility, or potential plan. It is time to answer the call of your soul.

For now, assume that all the resources you need to fulfill your mission—time, money, childcare, spousal approval, etc.—are already here. Use your natural powers of imagination to pretend for now that you have no material world concerns that are blocking you from saying yes. We will address these later.

However much the ego or inner critic may protest, simply say, "I hear you, and I thank you for sharing." Assume, for purposes of this exercise, that all of your needs are met. You are safe.

Remember that you are not trying to come up with a scenario. You are tuning into your heart. Your intention to sense, feel, visualize, or imagine your heart's knowing is the bridge to receiving guidance.

You might want to write down this intention:

I am playfully entering my imaginary world. I am open to receiving the perfect wise guidance for me and all concerned.

Now, as you let your pen move across the page, complete this sentence:

Wow! I just received a call from God (my higher self, my inner wisdom—or whatever term works best for you), directing me to …

Write in your journal as many details as come to you. If you are feeling challenged in sensing your guidance, do the following exercise, *Memory Magic*, first. This will infuse you with energy and move you back into your creative flow.

 Exercise: *Memory Magic*

One of my favorite exercises for shifting into a feel-good emotion is harnessing a positive memory. The subconscious mind does not know the difference between the present, past, or future, real or imagined. Therefore you can travel back and tune into a time when you felt relaxed, happy, peaceful, etc. By bathing in the energy of this memory, you return your body's chemistry to your true natural state: peaceful and at ease.

I have done this wonderfully healing exercise many times when I felt uncertain about my future. My spirit would often take me back to a time when I was in total bliss, nurturing my newborn daughter. Trust your spirit to bring you to the exact right memory that you need for your healing.

Taking in some deep breaths, close your eyes and allow yourself to relax. Put one or both hands on your heart. Feel your heartbeat. Now allow your heart, your spirit, to take you back to a time in your life when you felt relaxed and at ease. This might have been one isolated moment in time. Wherever your spirit takes you is perfect. Just allow yourself to be guided.

Once in your memory, let yourself fully relax and enjoy it. Take in the energy of this memory with all of your senses. See what is around you. Feel the warmth, the freedom, the peace—whatever emotion this memory is causing you to feel. Hear the sounds. Smell the scents. Let yourself taste the tastes. Feel your connection to this memory nourish every cell in your body. Bathe in these good feelings for as long as you desire. When you feel relaxed and revitalized, come back into present time.

I encourage you to come back to this exercise anytime you want to feel anchored in love and peace.

If you haven't yet done the previous exercise, *Imagining the Call*, I encourage you to go back and take the guided journey to sense what is calling you, before moving on.

Transforming Obstacles

No one answers the call without running up against inner and outer noes. The voice of resistance, whether it shows up as an inner critical dialogue or in the form of people who aren't cheering us on, is part of every hero's journey. For example, despite the strong sign of cosmic support I received from our New Mexico Car license plates, my former husband was not so enthused. Not only did he not share my excitement for the road trip, there was no pile of money sitting in our bank account to pay for the trip. So I continued to teach spirituality workshops in my living room and temporarily shelved the trip.

One day, I was going through my closet and found my EAT training materials, photographs, and mementos, including the Green Machine. I flashed back on how this magical implement had freed me during our training weekend.

After writing out our instructions from God, Jane said it was time to make our vision feel more real. We each took turns acting out our imagined call from God and our ensuing hero's journey. It was like theater in the round, within a safe circle of soul family cheering each other on. By bringing our calling to life, we could fully embody the visions that our souls had communicated through our imaginations.

Having a visceral experience of answering your soul's call is vitally important to making it part of your reality. Embodiment is key. Acting out your call, using movement, sound, action, and play, makes it much more likely that you will take the steps to act on your vision.

I laid out a red towel to resemble my new Honda and pretended to make the drive to Santa Fe, singing Avril Lavigne's "Complicated" at the top of my lungs.

Then I hit a roadblock. A curmudgeonly old man, resembling a troll, short with a gray beard and in a terrible mood, had literally blocked off the road, saying I could not proceed. He had no particular reason why I couldn't pass, but he was very set in his position.

I didn't argue with him. I didn't even try to reason with him or attempt to have him see things my way. I just began throwing my florescent Green Machine tennis ball up in the air.

"Keep your eye on the ball. Notice as it flies up to the sky, what happens," I instructed him.

He followed the Green Machine. "Wow!" he exclaimed, captivated. "It turns purple!"

"Exactly!" I said. "That's because it's magic!"

The more I threw the ball up, the more it changed colors. Orange, blue, yellow, and red! Now sparkles of light glowed around the ball.

My road-blocking troll was so enraptured by the colors and sparkles that his heart began to soften. Now he wanted to play too. He tossed the ball to the heavens several times. The more he looked up and saw the magical change of colors, the more he too began to shift his mood. Relaxing and starting to have fun, he began to laugh with delight.

The two of us tossed the Green Machine back and forth, up in the air and all around. After playing with me for a bit, he seemed to forget why he was blocking my forward movement. He smiled, opened the gate, and let me pass.

Standing in my closet, all of this passed through my mind as I remembered my phone call from God and divine direction to travel to Santa Fe. My heart lit up again at the thought of saying yes—even if I did not yet know how to make it happen.

Play Is the Way

As soon as we say yes to our dreams, the gatekeepers line up to block our way, as my friend the troll did. He had no reason to block my way but he didn't care—he wasn't going to let me pass for anything. That is, until I showed him the Green Machine and he began to relax and play with me.

This is how the inner critic, the voice of the scared ego, operates. Inner critics are like "No" people. To them, life is unfair, not fun, not worth living, and fraught with danger. There's always something to be afraid of, always a reason our dream won't work, and definitely a strong chance things will go wrong.

The critic refuses to give our sparks of possibility a chance because it lives in the consciousness of fear. To the critic, every idea or vision is a potential land mine. The critic often means well—it thinks its job is to protect us from harm—but it is misinformed. It is totally oblivious to the knowledge that we live in a loving Universe that is conspiring for our success. The critic also has no clue that our higher, wiser self, our soul, is guiding us. It kinks the flow of creative possibility like cutting off our breathing and oxygen flow.

Fortunately, we can turn our inner trolls into friends, or at least neutralize their impact on us. In truth, inner critics are nothing to fear: they are simply undernourished aspects of our unconscious that haven't received the love and care they need to feel safe and able in the world. They simply need our attention and loving presence.

For example, in my imaginary hero's journey, it was enough to engage my troll in play. This was the bridge that moved me into the wise space of my heart. Being light and playful took me into my imagination, where I could access a solution! I could decide that my magic implement had otherworldly powers of transformation. Engaging my childlike wonder freed me to see other options. Being trapped by the grumpy roadblocker was only a perception—a perception that shifted when I relaxed and engaged him in play. This is a powerful metaphor for life. Often, we feel stuck because we're stuck in the critic's land of no possibility. We need to get out of our narrow mindset, loosen up, do a little dance, or play a little ball.

All You Need Is Love: Let the Critic Rant

Sometimes getting into the right mindset isn't enough. The critic needs to be heard. It needs a chance to speak its mind. The critic needs nourishing and love. When we act like a caring parent and pause to observe and acknowledge its concerns, fears, and worries, we usually feel a palpable shift. The critic releases it's emotional hold on us and we are freed to move forward.

The inner critic speaks in many voices. The unifying thread is scarcity and fear. For the critic, something is always missing. Critics can show up as the Perfectionist, for whom nothing if ever good enough. Or the Procrastinator, who always has a reason to put off dreams or wait for a "better" time. Other times, it's the voice of Confusion, Doubt, or Worry. Or the biggie: Fear.

The following exercise will give the inner critic the loving attention it needs.

 Exercise: *Talk to Me*

Begin by allowing the critic to have a voice. Go ahead and let it rant. Observe the critic's rant like a nurturing parent who lovingly stands watch while their two-year old has a little tantrum. Ranting brings release. Release is healing. It ushers in a soothing calm after the storm.

First, identify the critic. Tune in to the situation or person that is bringing up inner criticism or other unpleasant emotions. Notice the tenor of the inner dialogue. Does it sound like the Perfectionist or the Procrastinator? Or the voice of Confusion, Doubt, or Worry? Give the inner critic a name.

The inner critic that is "up" for me right now is …

Next, allow the critic to express its thoughts, fears, and concerns. The inner critic often has ideas about what you should do or an opinion on what you are doing or not doing. Invite the critic to express herself.

For example:

> *My Dear Procrastinator,*
> *Please tell me what you have to say.*
>
> *Love,*
> *Betsy*

And the inner Procrastinator might answer:

> *Well, since you asked, I am exhausted! This project is way too stressful! As usual, you have too much on your plate and you're stressing me out—and everyone around you too. This has to stop. You've got to get your life under control. You do this rushing-around-like-crazy thing all the time. You don't need to add one more thing! This is not the time for this project. Wait a month or so when things are more manageable.*

Now you:

Invite the inner critic to share its thoughts and feelings with you. Listen to what it has to say and write it down.

It's time to soothe the critic. Don't skip this part. Responding to the critic as if you were a caring, nurturing parent is key to transforming the stuck energy into creative flow.

For example:

> *My Dear Procrastinator,*
>
> *Thank you so much for sharing your thoughts and feelings with me. I sooo hear you! I am so sorry you are feeling sad and angry about how this project has been going. I hear your concerns as well. I want you to know that you no longer need to protect me. I am in charge now. I am being guided and guarded by Spirit, by the voice of our soul. Together, we are keeping you safe. All is well.*
>
> *Love,*
> *Betsy*

Your turn:

Write a note to the inner critic, thanking it for sharing, acknowledging its concerns, and letting it know that you and your soul/wise self are in the driver's seat. You can come back and do this process any time you feel resistance to moving forward on your desires.

> *Dear* _____,

> *Love,*

Follow the Call ... One Clue at a Time

If your intention is to be guided, your destiny is always moving you forward, even when it doesn't feel like it. For example, I drove my shiny red Honda for some time before pointing it in the direction of Santa Fe. What I recall is feeling especially vulnerable around this time. Two years after the completion of my EAT training, I had begun to sense that my marriage was unraveling. Although I very much wanted to revive it, I was uncertain about our future. I had entered what many spiritual seekers call "the void," a place where life as you've known it is shifting.

In the void, you are living in a space of in between—you are between visions. One life chapter appears to be ending and the next one has yet to be written. An old life dream is dying and the new one has yet to be birthed. You sense that you are entering a time of major upheaval (or you may be in one now), but you have no idea where you're headed. The ground beneath you is moving—like it does when you are standing on a beach and the tide washes over your feet, softening and moving the sand beneath you. That your world may be permanently altered is terrifying to the ego—so you find yourself moving in and out of sometimes paralyzing fear and exhilarated possibility.

The beauty of this phase is that you are becoming more your true self. Your soul is gaining ground. A layer of your prior conditioning is melting away, freeing you to act more from your inner truth as you follow the call of your divine destiny. It often feels as though a part of you is dying, because in a way it is. Your old self, the part of you that wants to fit in, be liked, and please others, often to the detriment of your true destiny, is dying. More space is being made for your real, much more authentically powerful, self to steer your life, even if it feels like you are steering a homemade wooden canoe through a thick fog and can only see three feet ahead of you. This is why you may see no connection between the guidance you're given to make the next steps and your heart's desire.

I could have resisted, wondering how taking a road trip to New Mexico had anything to do with my dream to become a spiritual teacher. Where's the obvious connection there? But having said yes to my soul's guidance to try stand-up comedy and take the EAT training, I had begun to trust the calls of my soul.

I don't know anyone who has seen the full blueprint to their soul's destiny, complete with step-by-step directions. It's just not how life works. The ego wants to see its whole hand of cards now, *along with* the hands of all the players in our life. The ego wants to know the end of the movie before it even begins. The funny thing is, who would go see such a movie? We love the suspense of not knowing—unless, of course, it's *our* movie!

The soul knows that it's not the knowledge of what's next that propels us forward and infuses us with the hunger and motivation to live our movies in the first place. The soul has a healthy lust for the journey itself. It wants to feel and experience, embrace and engage, contribute and serve, delight and discover, adventure and dive, dare and stretch, reach and roam, even if that means getting lost in the process before being found again.

The soul knows that after we reach our target destination, there will be another, and another, leg of this wondrous journey of life ahead. Thus, we are given one clue to our destiny at a time. Spirit operates on a need-to-know basis.

If not now, who knows when I would take this trip? I felt the power of my spirit rising up within me. As I journaled daily asking for clarity, I heard the burning desire—characteristic of my soul's voice—come through. This primed the pump of my passion.

I began to feel a kind of "I don't care" feeling that sounded like:

> *I don't care if we don't have the money. I don't care if it doesn't make logical sense to take several days to drive to Santa Fe. I don't care if my husband doesn't want to go and I am the only driver for long stretches at a time. I've never before driven ten hours on end, but I can do it! I am going anyway!*

Letting my spirit and soul come through fueled my inner fire until I finally gave in to inspired desire and gave myself permission. I didn't yet know where the money would come from, but like my trip to Vail at the tender age of twenty-two, I was going. As soon as I committed, my heart caught fire with excitement, and creative ideas, resources, and support began to flow in. Maps materialized. Friends turned me on to amazing must-see national parks and places of spiritual power.

I experienced a synchronous stream of events akin to W.H. Murray's experience of his *Mount Everest Expedition*:

> Until one is committed there is hesitancy, the chance to draw back, always ineffectiveness. Concerning all acts of initiative (and creation), there is one elementary truth, the ignorance of which kills countless ideas and splendid plans: that the moment one definitely commits oneself, then Providence moves too. All sorts of things occur to help one that would never otherwise have occurred. A whole stream of events issues from the decision, raising in one's favor all manner of unforeseen incidents and meetings and material assistance, which no man could have dreamt would have come his way. I have learned a deep respect for one of Goethe's couplets: Whatever you can do, or dream you can, begin it. Boldness has genius, power and magic in it! [16]

Boldness in service of a sincere calling *does* activate magic. I felt the power of my bold decision supporting me.

I even came up with a way to include the whole family and give myself the time alone I needed to get a new perspective on my life and our marriage. I decided that even if my husband wasn't interested in a road trip, I could take my kids—one each leg of the trip that is. From divine enthusiasm, an ingenious solution emerged.

My husband, now open to vacationing in New Mexico (almost a miracle in itself), agreed to meet us in Santa Fe by plane with our youngest daughter, Molly. The oldest, Kate, accompanied me on the way there, and Molly was my travel partner on the trip back. This gave me special, one-on-one time with each of them, and I didn't have to negotiate the inevitable sibling conflicts. This made it a peaceful journey, giving me long stretches to think and just be while my sleep-loving daughters napped. And it gave my girls and me the joyful adventure of discovering some of the most beautiful places on earth together.

The Hidden Gifts of the Call

One of these places was Arches National Park, home to stunning red-rock arches and canyon walls that reach high into the vast crystal blue expanse of sky. One morning,

I woke up before dawn and arrived in the park just as the sun was rising. As far as I could tell, I was the only human being there, and I felt completely enveloped in the presence of life.

I began walking down some red-rock steps into an expansive ravine bordered by two mammoth rock walls. The sun was rising behind one of the walls, lighting up its edges with a soft glow. It was exceedingly quiet and still. In that moment, it felt like time had completely stopped. I felt as if the plant life, the canyon walls, the ground beneath me even, were all joining together to hold me in a symphony of rapturous love. Every element of nature, the air, the earth, the sunlight, was incredibly alive. I cannot describe the sheer beauty and magnitude of the spiritual presence I was feeling. I felt so in awe of the experience that I began to cry sweet tears of homecoming and joy.

In that moment, I became aware that all of the human conflicts we have, all of our worries, concerns, and burdens are completely inconsequential to our real purpose for being. They are simply the dramas we play out. Navigating our issues and concerns, we learn how to be with one another and with ourselves. We learn how to love. The dramas are just the stage on which we learn. Only the love is real.

As I felt waves of warmth open my heart with more and more love, I kept hearing the voice of my soul say, "*This* is why I came here. *This* is what I came to experience. *This is it!* This is the reason I'm here!"

This ecstatic heart opening continued as my girls and I toured stunning natural spots. Over and over, I found myself in total awe, feeling the most visceral connection to God and my own spirit that I had ever touched. Crying tears of gratitude became the norm for my journey. I felt as though I was having a love affair with Spirit, who was meeting me in the early morning hours of sunrise at each scenic destination on our itinerary.

The red rocks, crystal blue skies, and vibrant healing energy of Arches, Sedona, and Mesa Verde National Park deeply nourished me. To this day, I cannot describe with words the fullness of what I was given—to a degree it remains a divine mystery. What I do know is that the journey itself changed me. Driving on the sunny open road, I felt incredibly free and open to possibility. Every time I came to the crest of a hill, I felt a wonderful sense of expansion. Who knew what new vista was about to reveal itself on the other side. The exhilaration of wide-open vista after wide-open vista fortified me.

I was coming alive again.

And another hidden gem emerged: I received a *remembering* of the truth of who I was. I remembered my ability to make decisions independent of my husband, or any significant other for that matter. As long as I was tuned in to my heart and soul, I felt strong. I was out on my own, walking independently, but not feeling alone. The presence of my soul was palpable. I could feel Spirit very much with me. My tears of joy kept me very much in the now. In those moments, the gratitude and love was so full in my heart, there was no place for fear to enter. No room for aloneness to seep in.

I began to feel safe to let in the possibility of a life change.

Clearly, my Spirit was ushering me into a new beginning. I felt lifted by the freedom of forging my own path. Without realizing it, I was growing ready to say yes to the next nudge of my soul.

Every soul calling is an invitation. A hidden gift always awaits your yes! The ego will question even your most enthusiastic yes, and throw out its noes. To the intellect, taking action on the call makes no linear or logical sense. Your call will ask you to do something that takes you out of your usual mode—out of your comfort zone. It is only here, in new and wildly uncertain territory, that you will be awake enough, present enough, to see what you have been asleep to.

If imagining saying yes invigorates you, trust it.

Trust that any possibility that lights you up is your new beginning waiting to happen.

12

The Magic of Yes

Faith is a knowledge within the heart, beyond the reach of proof.

~ Kahlil Gibran

Today, show me the truth of who I am in every breath that I take. As I interact with others in this world full of beauty and love, allow me to see the everyday miracles right in front of me. Let me freely grieve what has left, and joyously celebrate what is arriving. Allow me to set down any burdens, knowing that all of my needs are met, and this is enough. Let me know that life, today, this moment, truly is a miracle.

~ A Journal Entry

I love the song "No Such Thing," in which John Mayer reveals the truth about life: that there's no such thing as "the real world."

There *is* a real world, but it's not the one we've been taught to believe in. Everything "real" in this world was initiated first with a thought in someone's imagination. Someone with their own story, their own perceptions, and their own beliefs. That someone is each of us. That someone is you. Today is the first day of the rest of your life. This is the first moment, the first breath, of the new beginning that awaits you. With your thoughts and feelings—with your imagination—you get to write the story, the script, of your new beginning. You are free to create your own *real*.

I remember a wonderful-feeling dream I had that filled me with renewed hope and possibility. In my dream, I was living in the same house I live in now, but one day, something miraculous happened. I was walking through my home and all of a sudden I noticed a hallway that I had never seen before. Of course I was curious, so I walked through it and found that it led to a whole additional wing on my house that I didn't know existed!

I walked through a doorway into a beautifully designed and comfortably furnished "great room" and kitchen. I saw my daughters, happily chatting away at the dining table. The gourmet kitchen had gleaming white cabinets and state-of-the-art appliances. Light poured in through the large picture window above the sink. Happy people walked by, smiling and waving hello through the window. Everything I saw in my new wing exuded warmth, love, and abundance.

In my dream, I felt ecstatic. I was stunned that these extra rooms had been there all the time—without me knowing it! I was in jaw-dropping awe about my new discovery. What I thought was true about something so intimate to me, my own home, was actually very different from reality. In my dream, my living quarters were much more expansive than I had previously known.

Dreams, of course, are communications from the unconscious, or the deeper part of us, the soul. The emotion that we feel while dreaming is, in my experience, the dream's primary message to us. I felt newly expansive, as though I had won the million-dollar lottery. I woke up with a clear sense of what my soul was telling me. If I could have received a text message from my soul about my dream, it would have read:

Dearest Beloved,

You are so much more than you can even comprehend. You have infinite possibilities available to you. You are abundant beyond what you have been sensing. Expand your vision to see the truth beyond your perceived limitations. Metaphorically speaking, you have rooms within you that you didn't even know existed! You think you are a comfortable two-bedroom house, when you are actually a gorgeous mansion with many wings. Regardless of appearances, you are an expansive being with infinite resources just waiting to be accessed.

We in Spirit are celebrating with you!
Your Loving Soul

I got it. My dream was saying this: Do not judge your potential by your current physical reality.

Trust that there is more to you, and your life's potential, than meets the eye. The "real-world" limitations that you feel are just what you see in this moment. That your bank account may be deficient or you don't have the love you desire or the economy is blocking you from getting your dream job—these are only perceptions. They are not truths.

What is true is that even if your outer circumstances are not what you fully desire, this does not have to limit you from creating more. You are an infinitely expansive and creative being. When you discover that you have more inner rooms than you realized, sunlit rooms with positive, loving energy, you awaken to the fact that *you are not your limitations.*

And once you hit on something you deeply desire and commit to it with your passionate *yes!*, you have ignited your potential to create a new reality—a wonderful new beginning.

Any possibility for a new beginning will most likely bring up ego fears and stories of "impossible." Fortunately, these are just stories, and stories can be rewritten and changed. With this awareness, you can consciously meet your fears with the truth: you are a naturally abundant creator with many rooms in your mansion. The extra wings in your ever-expanding quarters are just waiting to be inhabited as you say yes to the calling of your soul.

Expect Magic!

To bring a new dream to life, you have to let go of your old story—the story of who you think you are: a human being tied to a set of circumstances that cannot be changed or evolved to make room for what your heart desires. You need a new story of expanded possibility, such as:

> *The Universe is on my side. My deepest desires come from my soul. As I partner with my soul and listen to my inner guidance, the Universe supports me and meets me halfway. Everything I need to make my desire a reality is flowing to me now.*

For example, a couple of weeks ago, on Thanksgiving Day, my daughter Kate and I walked into my kitchen after an invigorating three-mile walk around Green Lake. Kate goes to college ninety minutes away, so she hadn't been home with me for a while. She asked me about a note hanging on the wall over my kitchen sink—something she hadn't seen before.

Three days earlier, I'd had a desire that I hadn't yet put out to the Universe. I wanted funding for a creative project. Specifically, an influx of cash to cover the publishing of this book! I had fallen into the rut of thinking the money had to come from a specific source such as my income or savings account. Not true, of course, but I was thinking inside a narrow box. I wanted to open the channels to receive funding from anyone, anywhere. I didn't want to cut off the flow by expecting it to come only from these places. I put some affirmative messages around my kitchen that read:

I always have plenty of money.

There is always money available when I need it.

Money is coming to me and for me from all directions.

This last note was the one Kate noticed on my wall. But she was struck by something else as well.

"Mama, I like the way you taped that money to your affirmation note," she said, pointing to a five-dollar bill taped to the message I had written to the Universe. I laughed, assuming that she had put the cash there and was playing and joking with me. She was adamant, however, that she hadn't. Since she had asked to borrow some money from me on our walk, it made sense that she wasn't my magical donor.

My heart warmed immediately. My affirmative prayer had been answered! Sure, it was only five dollars, but it felt symbolic of cash flowing to me in response to my request. Even more powerful was the sense that this was a communication from Spirit affirming that I was being supported. I was receiving a beautiful gift from the Universe, reminding me that life is conspiring for my success, on my side, ready to provide. Having this magical-feeling event occur on the Thanksgiving holiday made it feel that much sweeter.

For a moment, a possibility flashed in my awareness: what if it *wasn't* a human being who gave me this gift? I've read countless stories of people receiving "pennies from heaven," but I had never experienced anything this dramatic in my own life. What if this symbol of abundance was put there by an unseen spiritual helper, such as a guardian angel or my dad, with whom I've been consciously connecting and asking for support? Chills ran up and down my spine.

Neither Kate nor I had seen the cash on the wall prior to leaving the house for our walk. But just in case we'd missed it, I immediately went into detective mode, tracing my memory for who could have been in my kitchen in the last few days since I'd put the affirmation up. I narrowed it down to three possible people. They all swore they hadn't been my "money angel."

I may never know for sure, but whoever gifted me, the message was potent. When your desire is sincere and you remember to ask, the Universe will respond in some fashion. The part we forget is to open all the channels. To open our imaginations to the possibility that time, money, love, and the right people—all the resources we truly need—can come from any source. After all, Spirit is the source providing for us. The Universe has infinite means and streams to flow goodness our way—when we're open to seeing it!

Life wants to shower us with all that we can imagine and more.

Don't Be Fooled by Appearances

Not long ago, something fairly disturbing happened. I was driving under a freeway underpass, on my way to meet my coach, James, for a session. It was a warm Indian summer day, so my car window was down all the way. Suddenly a dirt clod came flying into my driver's side window, hit my left arm, exploded into pieces and covered me in black dust. It scared me to death. Luckily, a line of cars ahead of me was stopped at a red light, so I could safely brake and catch my breath. Although I can't imagine why anyone would want to throw any kind of projectile at me, I looked around to see where it had came from. I didn't see a single person.

I was grateful to be meeting with James so I could process what had happened. "I suppose it could have fallen down from the overpass," I offered.

James laughed.

"What are you laughing at?" I asked.

"Clearly," he said with a smile, "the Universe was trying to get your attention. If the clod had fallen down from above you, it would have come straight down, not horizontally through your car window."

"Well, I didn't see any person who could have thrown it," I responded.

He laughed again. "Betsy," he said with his rare ability to combine firm clarity with affection, "*the Universe* threw it at you!"

I still wasn't getting it: "Why? What for?"

"To wake you up!" he said, still laughing and now raising his voice another octave.

Just before that I had told James that the Universe seemed to be creating space for me to write my book. Around the same time, several clients had completed coaching with me. In the past when this happened, I usually attracted new clients to fill their places. I was worried about my income and feeling that something was wrong. Specifically, that I was *doing* something wrong. I was trying to make meaning out of it. "What do you think is happening?" I asked James.

My ego was dead set on coming up with an explanation. When something appears to be ending, leaving, or falling apart, egos want an explanation. So we attempt to create a story that "makes sense."

Meanwhile, my soul was quietly whispering, "Nothing is wrong. You're just getting space to finish your book. We are making room for your dream. *Relax.*"

This is what James was referring to when he stressed that the Universe was trying to get my attention. He was witnessing me fretting about my external circumstances. "As you teach your clients," he said, "figuring out *the why* isn't your business. If you want more clients, we can talk about that. But don't waste your energy creating a story about this."

I knew he was right. Being hit with the clod *did* get my attention.

I wasn't thrilled with the less-than-gentle way the Universe delivered its message, but I got it: "Wake up and see that anything shifting in your life is not the truth of who *you* are. Stay on track. Keep your eye on the prize. Finish your book."

And I give you the same advice. If something feels off from your normal life—if you're experiencing a loss—can you see where this is giving you space for a new beginning? Room for a new door to open?

Spiritual law dictates that chaos has to precede creativity. If you have a new open space that you did not invite, take heart. Every void must be filled with something new. Come back to your heart and remember your spirit. Return to your desires. Remember that you are opening to your divine destiny—to the plan of your soul.

The ego will always want to make up a story about your present circumstances. It will judge and look for what is wrong or missing. Do your best to withhold judgment. You may want to go back to the TLC Plan in Chapter Seven.

If you must make up a story, let it be an *empowering* one! Let it be that the Universe is making space for something magnificent to show up! Because it is. And for heaven's sake, don't listen to any stories about your life that don't lift you up, including your own.

Keep Your Eye on the Prize

I once had a fantastic mystical experience whose origin I cannot explain in anything but spiritual terms. I was lying on my bed one late afternoon, feeling very relaxed with my eyes closed. So relaxed that I was on the verge of dozing off, but I was still very conscious and aware. Suddenly, I felt my body vibrate as though I was lifting off. I had had this same feeling years before, but I got scared and stopped it from going past the rumbling. This time I sensed what was happening and I was excited. I consciously felt the fear while staying focused on the experience—on the excitement. Inside I said, Yes! Bring it on!

As I felt my body vibrate, I saw a picture in my mind's eye. It looked just like the gray lines of static on a television screen. In a flash, the static cleared and opened up to a movie playing on the screen. The next second I saw and felt myself *in* the movie. I began flying over a vast snowy terrain at high speed. The terrain was so unfamiliar that I sensed this was another continent or maybe even a different planet. Wow! As this was happening, I could feel the absolute awe and joy of knowing I was having a spectacular experience that I had never before had in my lifetime.

I became aware that I was having an out-of-body experience. Besides feeling the incredible rush of flying, what I remember most is the feeling that I wanted this to last forever. Some part of me knew, however, that the only way to keep it going was to stay intently focused on my flight—to literally keep my gaze on what was right in front of me. I sensed that if I turned my focus to something else or went into my intellect and questioned what was going on, the experience would end. I would come right back to this physical reality and lose my flight. If I had looked backward, I would have been plunked back down on my bed with a thud.

Like my new-wing house dream, this out-of-body episode gave me a huge boost of hope and joy. Once again, I received the clear message that life is not what it seems. So much more exists than we can see through our limited lens of perception—our everyday experience of life.

My transcontinental flight taught me a great lesson. It is so easy to get distracted by what isn't working in life. The ego wants to focus on fixing so-called problems—to change what feels missing or bad or wrong. What if every time an airplane hit turbulence, the captain made a U-turn and returned to the departure airport? Instead, the pilot keeps going, staying focused on the flight's destination, moving up to a higher altitude when necessary to fly with more ease.

If you turn your gaze and let yourself get distracted, the movie of your fabulous flight will stop. The way to stay in the flow is to adjust your altitude for turbulence and stay focused on where you're headed.

Keep your eyes on the prize of your desire.

Let the Universe Care for You

In western cultures, we are taught to aggressively go after our goals, work hard, and make things happen. Inspired action is part of bringing our dreams into being. But this is only one side of the equation. The other side is receiving. To manifest our hearts' desires, we have to become good receivers.[17]

Most of us weren't shown that giving and receiving are two sides of the same coin. So often we end up exhausted from putting out so much energy and then wonder why we're not getting back what we're giving. On top of this, many women and some men identify with being "givers." We have been raised and praised for helping others and sacrificing our own needs and desires. This kind of conditioning leads to feeling depleted and resentful. Generations of caregivers who've given until they collapsed have asked, "When is it going to be my turn?" We need a nourishing balance of giving and receiving. Becoming better receivers is key to creating happiness.

We are often given compliments, smiles, offers of support, and other gestures that we ignore or politely decline. For example, how many times do you tell a caring inquirer that you are fine when you are not feeling your best? This sends a message to the Universe and the subconscious mind that you are not really open to receiving support.

To receive what you desire, you need to tell a new story of yes! *Yes, I'm open! Yes, I'd be happy to receive help.*

With the intention to be a better receiver, you begin to see with new eyes. You've said yes to doing your part. Once you've asked for what you desire, you can expect answers to come. You're now open, aware, and accepting of support in all forms coming your way. I like to use this practice to expect great things—including magical-feeling experiences. What if you believed that something amazing is *always* on the verge of happening? This is a powerful intention, and it's also a fun way to live because it puts you on the lookout for something marvelous. It puts you in a place of happy expectation. Open, expecting, looking—this is when the magic happens.

With the intention to receive your blessings, you begin to look for them. You start to notice when things are coming to you. I suggest that you keep a *Yes* Journal to track your desires and all the many ways the Universe is answering your wishes and prayers. In your journal, log every positive gesture that you notice the Universe giving to you. This will make you a better receiver and open you up to delightful and serendipitous encounters that make your heart sing.

For example, after posting my affirmative messages about money coming to me from all directions and in all ways, I received a delightful gift in the mail. A career-coaching client who I hadn't seen for more than a year sent me an update, letting me know how happy she was in her job and volunteer work. With her note, she included ten coffee cards for free lattes at one of my favorite writing cafes. "Enjoy the beverage of your choice as you finish your book!" Her thoughtfulness and generosity lit me up and gave me a much-needed energy boost.

In my receiving journal, I write down gifts like this, along with gestures such as a compliment that made my day. When a client has a breakthrough that makes me want to shout, "Yes!" with elation, I write this down as well. Receiving and marking your wins allows you to be loved and nourished by your source. When you notice and document the goodness flowing to you, your story starts to change. You begin to live a new story of abundance.

You also become more aware of when you refuse an offer and vow next time to say yes. In the bigger picture, this is a practice of saying yes to all of life. Life wants to give to you, to nourish, love, and see you wildly successful and happy. If it's not happening, you can change your story. You can stop being stingy with yourself. You say yes first and watch the Universe begin to say yes in turn.

One more key to being a great receiver: *practice being honest about what you need.*

I have a client who told me she was ashamed of letting her extended community of family and friends know she was looking for a life partner because, in her words, it had been so long since her divorce. She was afraid of being judged, so she kept her desire under wraps. Unfortunately, this cut her off from both her loved ones and the flow. Many people meet compatible mates through family or friends. This is true for jobs that are a good match as well. Those who love you want to see you happy, just as the Universe does. They want you to have what you sincerely desire. To do this, you have to let them know what it is you're looking for!

This means giving up the image of yourself that you think others would prefer to the real you. It means being willing and vulnerable enough to share the current state of your life. You may judge yourself as flawed, unworthy, undeserving, and more, but you're actually more lovable when you're real. It's okay to admit that you don't have it all figured out. We all have things we're afraid to share for fear of others judging us. When you take the risk of being honest with others, you open up the flow and make yourself more available to receive your heart's longings.

Telling the truth to someone you trust usually brings great relief. You realize the thing you were most afraid to share isn't such a big deal. We're all human. We're all in the same life raft moving down the same river of life together. We need each other, and most of us sincerely want to support and help one another as well. When you tell someone what you need or desire, you give them a gift as well. You give them the gift of the true you. And the Universe hears this as, *I am ready to receive— bring it on!*

Be the Magician of Your Life

A few months ago, I added a new commitment with a steep learning curve to my life. I was very excited by the opportunity, but I also found myself feeling overwhelmed with extra work. I noticed that I began to wake in the morning and immediately go into *doing* mode. Do you ever notice yourself starting your day this way? Before you even leave your warm, cozy nest of a bed, you go into autopilot, creating a never-ending to do list? And feeling very burdened about it?

A lot of us do this by habit. The ego wants to feel in control, so before you even get out of bed (and sometimes in the middle of the night), the mind will start stressing over "everything I have to do." This is what the ego does to feel safe. It doesn't realize that it is just adding more stress and making us miserable before we've even had our first sip of morning coffee or tea.

This is a story too. It's the story of "Life is hard, stressful, _____ (you fill in the blank), and I have all of this to do."

It's not true. Yes, it may be true that you have a list of things you feel you need to accomplish. What isn't true, though, is that you have to feel heavy, burdened, anxious, or overwhelmed in the process. These feelings come from thinking that you have to do it all alone. You don't. You have help, and that help is your soul partner or higher self.

I use a tool that completely shifts the feeling I have about my day, even if I have a very full schedule or something that is triggering fear, doubt, or worry. It feels like a miracle technology, so I really want to encourage you to try it. Every time I do it, I get wonderful results. Using this technology, you can be the magician of your own life. Seriously.

Your greatest super power is your imagination. By engaging it and flowing your energy in the direction that you want to go, you get a much more positive result. For example, the other day I was beginning my day with a few hours of writing. Then I had two client sessions, including a couple I was counseling on Skype. Afterward, I had a little project using a computer program that was new to me, which caused me some anxiety.

Rather than getting up and powering through these varied activities, I chose the emotions I wanted to feel throughout my day. I wanted to feel joyful and at ease. So before rising, I closed my eyes, relaxed my body, and imagined myself moving through each activity feeling joyful and at ease. I saw myself writing well and feeling satisfied. I envisioned connecting with my clients and all of us feeling nourished and wonderful after our time together. I even imagined myself happily working with the new technology, finding that it was surprisingly easy to use and the project was successful. As a result of taking myself through this visioning process, my day turned out beautifully, just as I had envisioned it.

What I was doing was putting myself in the energy of my natural flow. We each have all the resources we need to move through our tasks and relate to obstacles with much more ease and flow than we often experience. Why? Because this flow is naturally abundant. It's like a stream of *yes* energy that meets us where we are and takes us where we want to go. It contains what we need. This is why we feel so good when we are in it. We call it being in the zone or losing track of time.

The key is choosing and feeling the emotion you want to feel—ahead of time. You are actually activating this emotion with your imagination. Imagining feeling wonderful sometimes feels like a stretch. Especially if the thing you're envisioning doing is triggering a stressful response. Like my computer activity, making me feel anxious. I can shift this by first noticing what emotion I *am* feeling. "Here I am, feeling stressed out and anxious about using this new computer program that I've only used once before … and had trouble with." Once I acknowledge the emotion, in this case anxiety, and let myself meet it, I can choose to flow my energy in another direction. I can intentionally imagine myself doing the activity really well and easily and feeling fantastic instead.

I say that by doing this flowing exercise, you are acting as the magician of your life, because it can really feel like magic! Your true nature is to feel great. When you feel emotions like worry or anger, it's because you are resisting your natural well-being. People refer to this resistance as hitting a wall, running into a boulder, or finding yourself between a rock and a hard place.

When you flow your energy in the way you desire to feel instead, you are a lot less likely to encounter obstacles. And if you do, you're a lot more likely to flow through them like a river flowing over or around boulders. In effect, you are dissolving any resistance between the result you desire and the environment you are interacting with. Intentionally bringing in your desired emotion—and really letting yourself feel it in your imagination—you set up a stream of well-being that you can relax into and float down.

This is the difference between walking around carrying a heavy burden on your shoulders and letting *life* carry you instead.

As I mentioned earlier, this is being in the *love flow*.

In a nutshell, the process is: You, expecting the best, plus imagining yourself experiencing the best. You are seeing, sensing, and feeling the outcome you desire in your imagination. Before you even get out of bed. Creating a warm river of good-feeling flow.

This is letting life carry you, instead of you trying to carry life.

All of which is tantamount to telling a new story: *I am the magician of my life. I flow my energy in the direction of my desires. And I feel amazing!*

 Practice: *Activate Your Inner Magician*

This is a simple practice to put yourself in the *love flow* of your soul:

- Before getting out of bed or during your morning meditation, choose an intention for how you want to feel in all of your activities. Make sure your intention is what you desire … what you are going toward rather than what you want to avoid. For example: *I am happy and free.*

- Now travel into your imagination, bringing your intention for the emotion you are choosing to activate. Sense, see, feel, hear, even taste the activities of your day. Imagine going through each of your activities one by one, consciously feeling the emotion you are intending. Feel this fully as though you are actually having the experience now.

- Go about your day, knowing that you have co-created a flow of positive energy corresponding to your intention. Enjoy the magic!

Be Open to Something Better

It turns out that the Universe supported me abundantly during the writing of this book. I traveled to Puerto Vallarta three times, and the last two trips were almost free. My dad's friend Ray generously offered me his condo for my third trip. And my mom, a retired airline employee, put me on her flight passes, so I was able to fly standby at no charge.

As serendipitous as all these gifts were, flying standby can be stressful because you never know for sure if you'll get on the flight. In my travels to and from Vallarta, I became accustomed to getting on, often receiving the last seat. With this divine assistance, I strongly felt the Universe conspiring for my success.

I felt very much in the flow, until I hit a snag on the second leg of my trip home from Washington Dulles to Seattle. Apparently, an earlier flight to Seattle had been canceled and a number of stranded *paying* passengers were lining up to get a seat on my flight. Since they get first priority, I began to feel nervous. The ticket agent at the gate was clearly stressed out as so many people were waiting in line, vying for just a few available seats.

I got a strong feeling that I wasn't going to get on this flight and started to feel my heart contract. I felt the familiar feeling of disappointment. When my sense was confirmed and they closed the plane door and the flight took off, I approached the ticket agent for help. She was still so upset from the stress of the flight that she refused to even look up at me while I waited patiently to get her attention. I went into fear, worried that I wouldn't get the help I needed to get on another flight that evening.

Then I remembered to stop and pray. One door had closed (literally!), which meant another one had to open. This is universal law. Where one opportunity vanishes a void is created that must be filled with a new one. *Dear Spirit,* I prayed, *show me where the new opening is. Show me my new flight plan.*

It turned out there was another flight home just one hour later. The agent, still visibly agitated, was now willing to at least direct me to the new flight. When I arrived at the gate, the energy in the air was palpably different. No one was waiting in line, and this gate agent was serene and upbeat, greeting me with a smile. "I have your boarding pass right here," he said, "but if you want to hang out for a few minutes, I might be able to get you on first class." "Oh, I think I can wait five minutes for that," I said, smiling to myself.

As I settled into my extra-wide window seat, appreciating the open aisle seat next to me for added comfort, the first-class cabin flight attendant handed me a refreshing preflight drink. I smiled at how the Universe was once again delivering this lesson. I had made a plan that my ego believed was "the one that had to be." I had forgotten that the Universe, by foiling my ego's plan, was surely doing its thing, rearranging the order of circumstances so that I could receive something even better. I had forgotten that I could trust in a bigger plan. Once again, the Universe was handing me evidence that it is safe to relax and go with the flow. *Celebrate this gift!* Spirit encouraged, as I documented it in my *Yes* Journal. *Count your blessings and write about the joys of your trip. We love you!*

When your hopes are dashed, it is very difficult to see the proverbial pot of gold at the end of the rainbow. It takes a conscious awareness and decision to shift your focus so that you can open to receive something different from what the ego, with its limited sight, can envision.

The trick is to remember to get back in the flow when circumstances trigger you into feeling dejected, rejected, or lost. My friend Allen has just one mantra that always works for him: "Get back in the river." I imagine the way water flows down a river, just because that's what water does. It washes over boulders, winds through bends, and manages to find its way downstream just by being its natural self. Like the river, there's always a flow happening within you, available for connection. You can imagine that you're stepping back into your life raft and floating gently, fully protected and carried by the stream of life.

Can you imagine that divine timing is orchestrating the best for you? When your desires don't seem to be manifesting, try to remember this: The Universe may just be working on putting you in first class.

Trust the Flow

Back at our EAT hero's journey weekend, our facilitator, Jane Goldberg, played a game with us. We had each acted out our hero's journey. I had traveled to Santa Fe and felt the exhilaration of freedom and the wind in my hair.

"Now," Jane said, "It's time to meet your future self."

Your future self is the new you that emerges from answering the call of your soul. It's your butterfly emerging from the chrysalis, the phoenix rising from the ashes. It's you, flying free, soaring on the wind beneath your wings.

Before the game, Jane took us on a guided meditation to meet our future selves. A meditation that went something like this:

Close your eyes and let your body and mind fully relax.

Breathe in some nice deep breaths.

On the exhale, let go and relax even more.

Allow yourself to go to that very relaxed state you go at night, just before you fall asleep.

Now imagine that you are in a beautiful, peaceful place in nature. Find yourself sitting next to a tree, your spine leaning against the trunk for support. In a few moments, you will see, sense, feel, or imagine the presence of your future self coming out from behind your tree. Soon this presence will make itself known to you. Close your eyes where you are and count to six. At the count of six, the appearance of your future self, the you that you are becoming, will make itself known to you. One, two, three, four, five ... and six. Become aware now of your future self. If you knew, who would she be? What would he look like? How would she act?

What would be important to your future self? Allow yourself to take in as much information as you can sense from this aspect of you. What is his or her heart's desire? His or her passion? What work is she or he doing?

We all came back from the meditation and wrote a description of the future self we met on our guided journey. (I encourage you to go on your own inner adventure as described in this meditation. When you come out, describe your experience on paper.)

Next, it was time for the game.

"You are all invited to join me," she said, "all of you as your future selves. Please be my guest on Jane's Talk Show. I am going to interview each of you. Come prepared to share your hero's journey—your phone call from God and what you are doing now as your future self. What has transpired since you said *yes* to the call of your soul?"

I loved this exercise. It was light and playful. Like kids pretending, we were encouraged to have fun and make it up. What would you do if you had no limits? If all of your needs were taken care of?

And that question we life coaches love to ask, because it's a good one:

> *What would you give yourself permission to do, if money, resources,*
> *and time were not at issue?*

I loved the game because I felt the voice of my soul come through loud and clear, with no effort on my part to come up with something. I just relaxed and handed the questions over to my imagination. I opened myself to whatever wanted to bubble up. I knew that I wanted to do work in the healing arts as a spiritual guide, but exactly what that was, I wasn't sure.

When Jane interviewed me, I found myself enjoying being on her talk show, bursting with new possibilities for my future. A new story emerged—a story that both delighted and surprised me. "So you're back from New Mexico," she said. "And what are you doing now?"

Staying in the flow and just speaking what came to me in the moment, I responded, "Oh, I am having the best time! I'm writing a book now, and I even have my own radio show! Yes, I am an author and spirituality talk show radio host."

Everyone supported me with joyful laughter. I could feel in their voices, in their eyes, that they believed this could happen. Acting it out, I too felt the possibility of my dream coming true.

That was eleven years ago, and now here I am, completing my book. Every Monday at noon, I host a radio show called *Just Say Yes!* The show is about freeing yourself to follow your divine destiny. Who knew? My soul knew, because it has my plan. Your soul knows the truth of your divine destiny.

If you had asked me then how long it would take to realize this dream, I proba-bly would have shrugged my shoulders. "A year or two would be awesome," I might have said, gleaming. But the Universe has it's own timing. As much as I would have wanted to throw my weight around and issue a timeline and ultimatum to Spirit, it would have been me planning, cajoling, and God turning toward me and laughing, compassionately, of course. And then saying:

> *Beloved, relax. You can let go now. Enjoy the ride. The timing isn't*
> *up to you to decide.*

Which reminds me of the song I've been hearing in my head since I began writ-ing these pages. "The Climb," [18] passionately sung by Mylie Cyrus, teaches us not to get stuck in striving to "make it" ... "to get somewhere." Because there *is* no *there*.

After your brilliant new beginning, there will be another one. And another. There will always be another mountain to scale. So take your time and enjoy the climb.

You open yourself to receive the call of your soul. You ask and listen. With your trusted wise guidance by your side, you are led. An answer, a clue, a sign, or synchronicity gives you an inspired whoosh of yes! You follow your guidance one small step at a time. Emerging from the darkness into the light, looking around this new frontier, you realize that you are new again. You have become real. More radiant than before. More fully and completely alive than ever.

You have done the one thing you came here to do: *become your true self.*

> *This is the magic of saying yes.*

Acknowledgments

I must first thank my deepest confidante, teacher, and co-creator, Spirit, for your constant and unconditionally-loving presence in my life. Words could never convey my overflowing gratitude for the guiding wisdom I continually receive from you.

To my clients, workshop participants, and radio listeners, everything I have learned from you is woven into these pages. Thank you from the deepest place in my heart for your trust and for our sacred partnership.

To my mom, Sandy Gutting, thank you for your love and support. You have taught me, by example, to see life through the eyes of an artist. To my dad, Gene Guy Gutting, thank you for standing by me in spirit.

I send my forever love and appreciation to my daughters, Kate and Molly, for always believing in me and for teaching me how to love unconditionally.

I am hugely grateful to my soul sister, Shelley, for always being there for me through life's storms and celebrations. Your editing contribution went way beyond the call of duty.

To Wendy, I am so thankful for your humor, your incredible support, and your presence in my soul family.

To Dave Benham, my prayer partner and sounding board, thank you for keeping me well fed and making me laugh.

To David Longmire, I am so blessed by your friendship and your generous assistance during my workshops.

For ongoing emotional and spiritual support, I am enormously grateful to Lorinda Siggins-Rainwater, Anthony Molinero, Laila Atallah, Sharon Greene-Stevens, Joline El-Hai, Kathleen Carerra, Tina Schermer Sellers, Lex Cooper, Kate Thompson, Irina Borshevskaya, Joseph "Bear" Baranowski, John Hooper, Mike Fischer, Steve Van Beek, Helen Maio, Steve Potts, Fred West, Allen Cudahy, Laura Lavigne, Don Beaty, and Sharon Ramey.

To Amber Pearce, thank you for your loving, generous spirit and the amazing gift of your research.

To Mark Husson, I am hugely appreciative of your ongoing support. Thank you for believing in me as a radio host.

For your comfort, advice, encouragement, and healing, thank you to Jan Santora, Rick Jarow, John Joseph, Darren Weissman, Denise Linn, Dr. Christiane Northrup, Sonia Choquette, and Suzanne Holmes.

Although I have had little or no personal contact with the following mentors, their books and presentations have inspired me and given me profound healing: thank you Barbara Sher, Gail McMeekin, Julia Cameron, Henriette Anne Klauser, Shakti Gawain, Alan Seale, John Welwood, Stephen Levine, Bill Plotkin, Daphne Rose Kingma, Neale Donald Walsch, Maria Nemeth, Laura Day, Robert Holden, Alan Cohen, Michael Bernard Beckwith, Rickie Byars Beckwith, John O'Donohue, Don Miguel Ruiz, Thich Nhat Hanh, Louise Hay, and Wayne Dyer.

To Jane Goldberg and the EAT tribe, I send loving appreciation. You created the cocoon that kept me safely held and nourished while my new self was incubating.

To Gail Ferguson, I feel extremely blessed by your honesty, intelligence, and encouraging presence.

To my coach, James Dunn, I am grateful for your humor, clarity, and presence.

To Doris Roach, thank you for reflecting back my light in moments of darkness.

Special thanks to Susan Crockett for your caring and for your rescue mission.

To my "angel" English teacher at UC Santa Barbara, thank you for your gift of encouraging my writing.

To Ray, thank you for blessing me with the generous gift of your Puerto Vallarta writing haven and for sharing your memories of my dad.

To Brian and Ben, I am deeply grateful for you and our joyful reunion.

To Dani, thank you for taking me under your nurturing wing in Vallarta.

To SARK, you gave me the magical gift of your beautiful believing eyes as the book was being formed. I am so grateful.

To Steve Bonnell, warm thanks for your bright and always supportive presence at East West Bookshop, Seattle.

And finally, to the team that helped me put it all together—editors Shelley Cochran, Suzie Hollingsworth, Sharon Reitman, and John Eckard; interior book designer Amy Pogue; cover artist Kate Warinsky; consultant Wendy Wilson; and web assistant extraordinaire Kara Jones—thank you for helping to birth this baby into the world.

Betsy Gutting
Seattle, Washington

 # Notes

Chapter One

[1] *The Top Five Regrets of the Dying: A Life Transformed by the Dearly Departing*, by Bronnie Ware (Carlsbad, CA: Hay House, 2011).

Chapter Two

[2] From *Women Food and God: An Unexpected Path to Almost Everything*, by Geneen Roth (New York: Scribner, 2010).

[3] *Friendship with God: An Uncommon Dialogue*, by Neale Donald Walsch (New York: Berkley Trade, 2002).

Chapter Three

[4] See The Institute of HeartMath Research Center. These research findings came from the e-book *Science of The Heart: Exploring the Role of the Heart in Human Performance—An Overview of Research Conducted by the Institute of HeartMath*. http://www.heartmath.org/research/science-of-the-heart/head-heart-interactions.html.

[5] According to Gregg Braden in *The Spontaneous Healing of Belief: Shattering the Paradigm of False Limits* (Carlsbad, CA: Hay House, 2008), feeling the positive emotions of desire creates patterns in the heart's magnetic and electrical fields. The energy patterns created from feelings are much stronger than those derived from thoughts. Positive feelings flowing from a genuine heart's desire send out a more powerful magnetic energy than thoughts alone. The Universe responds to the heart's powerful magnetic field by mirroring back the essence of what we desire.

[6] From *The Conquest of Fear*, by Basil King (New York: Garden City Publishing, 1921).

[7] If so, you might really enjoy the book, *F**K It Therapy: The Profane Way to Profound Happiness*, by John C. Parkin (Carlsbad, CA: Hay House, 2012).

Chapter Five

[8] *The Vortex: Where the Law of Attraction Assembles All Cooperative Relationships*, by Esther and Jerry Hicks (Carlsbad, CA: Hay House, 2009). See also, Ask and It Is Given: Learning to Manifest Your Desires, by Esther and Jerry Hicks (Carlsbad, CA: Hay House, 2004).

[9] We can understand the term, *frequency* in the context of a radio broadcasting tower. When we tune the radio to a specific station, we pick up the specific frequency or signal the station is putting out. For example, I enjoy music played on *The Mountain*, which comes in on 103.7 FM. I cannot expect to hear the radio frequency that is being broadcast from *The Mountain* on my tuner when I set it at 105.6. The vibrational frequencies must match.

Chapter Six

[10] *I Could Do Anything If I Only Knew What It Was: How to Discover What You Really Want and How to Get It*, by Barbara Sher (New York: Dell, 1995).

Chapter Eight

[11] See Obituary for Gabrielle Roth: http://uwgpsychology.org/2012/obituary-gabrielle-roth. The original, printed source of Roth's words could not be found before this manuscript went to press.

[12] *The 12 Secrets of Highly Creative Women: A Portable Mentor*, by Gail McMeekin (San Francisco, CA: Conari Press, 2000).

[13] According to neuroscientist Kelly G. Lambert, author of *Lifting Depression: A Neuroscientist's Hands-On Approach to Activating Your Brain's Healing Power* (Basic Books, 2008), "When you knit a sweater or plant a garden, when you prepare a meal or simply repair a lamp, you are bathing your brain in feel-good chemicals and creating a kind of mental vitamin. Our grandparents and great grandparents, who had to work hard for basic resources, developed more resilience against depression; even those who suffered great hardships had much lower rates of this mood disorder. But with today's overly-mechanized lifestyle we have forgotten that our brains crave the well-being that comes from meaningful effort."

Chapter Nine

[14] *Anam Cara: A Book of Celtic Wisdom*, by John O'Donohue (New York: HarperCollins, 1997).

Chapter Ten

[15] I first learned about this concept from Julia Cameron, author of *The Artist's Way: A Spiritual Path to Higher Creativity* (New York: Jeremy P. Tarcher/Putnam, 1992). In her seminal book on creativity, Cameron coined the word *crazymakers*, and details how to spot crazymakers and their destructive behavior.

Chapter Eleven

[16] W. H. Murray, *The Scottish Himalayan Expedition* (London: J. M. Dent & Sons, 1951). According to Meredith Lee, University of California, Irvine (5 March 1998), the Goethe couplet, which Murray refers to here is from an extremely loose translation of Goethe's Faust lines 214-30 made by John Anster in 1835. See http://www.goethesociety.org/pages/quotescom.html.

Chapter Twelve

[17] In her brilliant book, *The Power of Receiving: A Revolutionary Approach to Giving Yourself the Life You Want and Deserve* (New York: Tarcher/Penguin, 2010), author Amanda Owen goes into great depth about learning how to receive.

[18] "The Climb" is a song performed by American recording artist and actress Miley Cyrus for the 2009 film *Hannah Montana: The Movie*. The song was written by Jessi Alexander and Jon Mabe, and produced by John Shanks.

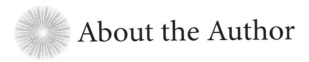 # About the Author

Betsy Gutting is an Intuitive Life Coach who leads workshops internationally and hosts a weekly online radio show called *Just Say Yes!* Seventeen years ago she left a law career to empower others to answer their heart's true calling.

Betsy has been offering transformational private coaching sessions and seminars for over a decade. She is also the creator of the powerful audio CD, *Guided Meditations for Awakening Your Passion*, which has catalyzed breakthroughs for many.

She lives in Seattle, Washington, where she loves to dance, make art, and savor time with her daughters.

Visit the author's website at **www.betsygutting.com**.

Made in the USA
San Bernardino, CA
28 May 2014